VIRGIL
AENEID II

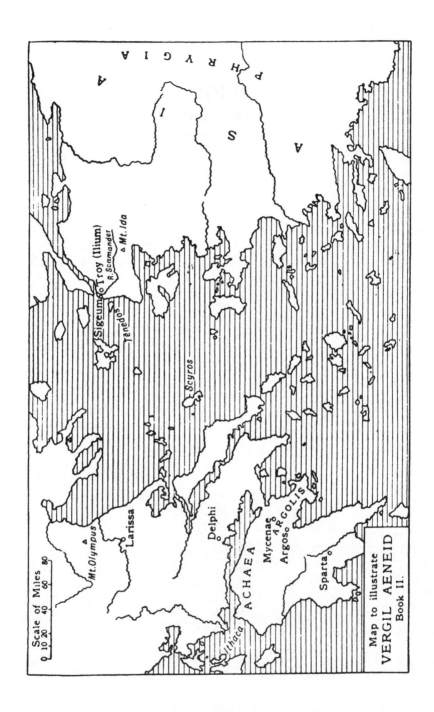

Map to illustrate
VERGIL AENEID
Book II.

VIRGIL

AENEID II

Edited with Introduction,
Notes and Vocabulary by

R.H. Jordan

Bristol Classical Press

To

MICHAEL BOOKER

saepe ego longos
cantando puerum memini me condere soles
Virgil *Ecl*. IX 51-52

This impression 2008
First published in 1999 by
Bristol Classical Press
an imprint of
Gerald Duckworth & Co. Ltd.
90-93 Cowcross Street, London EC1M 6BF
Tel: 020 7490 7300
Fax: 020 7490 0080
inquiries@duckworth-publishers.co.uk
www.ducknet.co.uk

A catalogue record for this book is available
from the British Library

ISBN 978 1 85399 542 2

Printed in Great Britain by
CPI Antony Rowe, Chippenham

CONTENTS

FOREWORD

This book of the Aeneid is one of the three most frequently read and enjoyed by those who are beginning their study of Latin poetry. This edition therefore has been designed to be of use in particular to both GCSE and A level students. The Introduction deals briefly with Virgil's life and various topics related to the poem as a whole; a select bibliography is also provided. There is a full Vocabulary, and the Notes are designed in the first place to give help with translating the Latin but also contain some pointers towards gaining an appreciation of the poetry.

The two Appendices provide help with Virgil's metre and the scansion of the lines, but it is hoped that the Latin will be read aloud. To ignore the sound of the poetry is to lose much of its force and even some of its meaning.

The text used in the preparation of this edition is substantially that to be found in the Oxford Classical Text of F.A. Hirtzel (1900). Any change to this resulted from consulting the valuable commentary in R.D. Williams' edition, *The Aeneid of Virgil* Books I-VI (London, 1972).

I owe a personal debt of thanks to a number of people: to my colleague Michael Harrison who read portions of the volume; to Colin Kirkpatrick and Vivienne Napier for their patience and help with word-processing; to my former colleague John McNee who gave me valuable advice on the Bibliography and made many valuable suggestions for the Notes. A special word of thanks must also go to Dr. Tony Sheehan of The Queen's University of Belfast for constructing a macro especially for the list of Proper Names.

Finally, may I thank the Bristol Classical Press, in the first place for giving me the opportunity of setting down my thoughts about this enthralling poetry, and for the help and encouragement of Jean Scott, the Managing Editor.

This volume is dedicated to Michael Booker, formerly Classics Master at Bristol Grammar School, who patiently guided my youthful and faltering attempts to understand and appreciate Latin poetry. A small recompense indeed.

R.H.J.
Belfast.

INTRODUCTION

Life of Virgil

Publius Vergilius Maro – better known by the anglicised form of his gentile name as Virgil – was born near Mantua in northern Italy on October 15th 70 BC. His father is said to have been a small farmer but he must have been not without means since his son, after primary education in Cremona and Mediolanum (Milan), studied Greek at Neapolis (Naples) and philosophy and rhetoric at Rome. It seems that he then returned home on the completion of his education and may have written minor works such as *Ciris, Copa* and others.

After the defeat of Brutus and Cassius at Philippi in 42 BC, Virgil's father was evicted from his farm. The youthful poet, however, won the favour of Asinius Pollio, governor of Cisalpine Gaul, to whom he dedicated his first major work, the ten *Eclogues*, pastoral poems imitating those of the Greek poet Theocritus. Pollio introduced Virgil to Octavian, the future emperor Augustus, as a result of which the family farm was possibly restored.

Virgil now lived mostly at Naples. He had become a friend of the emperor and a member of the exclusive set which gathered round the great literary patron Maecenas. Virgil followed the *Eclogues* with four books of *Georgics* that dealt with farming, livestock, trees and bee-keeping. These were not merely compilations of advice for farmers but an artistic masterpiece showing Virgil's love of the countryside and his mastery of the hexameter metre. The 2184 lines took him seven years to write, so carefully was each line polished and revised.

Virgil's great epic, the *Aeneid*, which is discussed below, was commissioned by Augustus himself and occupied the last eleven years of Virgil's life. He died at Brundisium (Brindisi) on his way home from a visit to Greece in 19 BC and was buried at Naples. The *Aeneid* had not received its finishing touches and the poet wished it to be destroyed. Augustus forbade this and ordered the poem to be published.

We know little of Virgil's personal life. Technically he was born a Gaul, for the people of Cisalpine Gaul only later received Roman citizenship. In the Middle Ages he was considered to be a sort of wizard; his fourth *Eclogue* was cited as evidence for this, since that poem was interpreted in part as a prophecy of the birth of Christ. Men seeking guidance about the future sought his advice by opening his works at random. Virgil himself was a shy, introverted person who seldom visited Rome and once, we are told, ran into a nearby house to avoid a crowd who had recognised him. And yet the poet Horace, whose character was in every way the opposite of Virgil's, counted him as a very dear friend – 'half of my life' he calls him. We can imagine him, in the quietness of his Neapolitan home, working on his great epic year after year, burnishing his brilliant hexameters and, in the end, dying not totally satisfied with his efforts.

The *Aeneid*

The *Aeneid* is a great national epic in twelve books telling how Aeneas, a Trojan prince, and other survivors from the destruction of Troy by the Greeks in the Trojan War left their homeland and sailed westwards to found a new city that would become more famous than Troy itself. In this Virgil was greatly influenced by the poems of Homer (see 'Virgil and his Predecessors' below). The first six books are largely taken up by the wanderings of the refugee Trojans and could be termed Virgil's *Odyssey*. The second half of the poem, Virgil's *Iliad*, concentrates on the warfare by which the Trojans established themselves in their new homeland.

Book I of the poem does not open with the Trojans sailing away from their burning city; instead it plunges into the middle of the story when after seven years of wandering the Trojan ships are caught up in a storm aroused by the goddess Juno and are driven towards the north coast of Africa. Neptune intervenes to calm the storm and ensure that the ships, though scattered, reach shelter. Aeneas gathers up his dejected followers and after learning from his mother, Venus, where they are, he leads them to the city of Carthage. Here they are welcomed by Dido, the queen, who lays on a lavish banquet for her guests at the end of which she asks Aeneas to tell her the story of his wanderings.

Book Two

Book II does not deal with his wanderings at all, but is the necessary prelude to his description of them. The poet relates how the Greeks, after so many years of fruitless warfare, finally devise the cunning scheme to gain entry to the city and take it by storm. The book opens with the construction of the huge wooden horse and the withdrawal of the Greeks to the island of Tenedos until the signal is given to say that the city has been seized. The Trojans now, with their enemies gone, are unsure what to do with the huge horse; Laocoon, the priest of Apollo, tries to warn them that it is a trick but there appears on the scene the deceitful Sinon. A Greek, he had deliberately stayed behind and allowed himself to be captured so that he could convince the Trojans that they had to take the wooden horse into their city. Finally, as though to reinforce Sinon's story, Laocoon and his sons are destroyed by two sea snakes sent by Pallas Athena. As ever, the great gods and goddesses take part in the unfolding events on one side or the other. So, with great celebrations the Trojans breach the walls of Troy and drag the huge horse into the city and place it on the citadel. That night as the celebrations die away the Greek warriors inside the horse emerge and set about securing the city and open the gates for their returning comrades. Aeneas himself now enters the story. The dead Hector appears to him in a dream to warn him that Troy's doom has been sealed and tell him to seek another city across the sea. Aeneas wakes up and in rage at the destruction going on around him rushes out to join the fray, despite the warnings of Hector. He gathers together a group of Trojans who disguise themselves in captured Greek armour and roam about putting up what resistance they can. They eventually retreat to Priam's palace. Here a series of events takes place which culminate in the deaths of Polites, Priam's son, and of Priam himself. In the palace Aeneas catches sight of Helen, who had been the cause of the war, and infuriated he determines to kill her. He is distracted by Venus, however, who appears before him and asks why he has abandoned his own father, wife and son. Aeneas now turns his attention to the protection of his own family. He goes in search of his father, Anchises, only to find that he obstinately refuses to leave the burning city; in frustration Aeneas is about to return to the hopeless fight but is detained by Creusa, his wife. There then occurs a strange omen; the hair of Aeneas' son appears to be on fire but the child is not harmed. As a result of this miracle, Anchises agrees to leave. Aeneas then lifts his father onto his shoulders and holding his son by the hand sets out; Creusa follows some distance behind. Aeneas arrives at the agreed rendezvous outside the city but finds that Creusa is missing. Leaving his father and son there, he returns to search for his wife. He is met by Creusa's ghost who tells him that Jupiter would not allow her to leave Troy with him. She then prophesies that he will travel a great distance over the sea to a land where the river Tiber flows through fertile fields to the sea. She assures Aeneas that she is not destined to be taken away as a slave by the Greeks. Aeneas returns to his family to find that many more have joined them; all together they set off for the mountains.

The Sequel

Book III continues Aeneas' story with a narrative of the dangers encountered by the refugee Trojans as they set off on their search for the land that has been promised to them. They visit Thrace, Delos and Crete before learning that Italy is their real destination. They travel on westwards to Epirus before turning south to Sicily. Throughout this voyaging Aeneas is guided and encouraged by Anchises. Finally Anchises dies at Drepanum in western Sicily and is buried there. At this point Aeneas ends his narrative.

Although Aeneas had at various times nearly given up his destined course, it is in Book IV that he comes closest to forgetting his mission. Dido, a widow and a refugee like Aeneas, falls in love with her guest and is attracted by the idea of inviting the Trojans to join her people and making Carthage a joint foundation. In this she is encouraged by Aeneas' mother, Venus. Without a thought for his destiny, Aeneas spends the winter months with Dido until Jupiter intervenes and warns him that he must leave Africa and fulfil his mission. He tries to leave in secret but Dido discovers that preparations are being made and she begs him to stay. Unmoved by her entreaties, Aeneas sails away and Dido commits suicide.

Book V tells how Aeneas returns to Sicily to celebrate the anniversary of his father's death with funeral games and much of the book is taken up with the description of these. However, it is during the games that another attempt is made to deflect Aeneas from his destiny. This time it comes from within his own followers; the women are now utterly weary of travelling and so, incited by Juno, they set fire to the ships in an effort to force Aeneas to abandon his mission and settle in Sicily. Jupiter sends a sudden rainstorm and quenches the fire. Only four ships are destroyed. The Trojans then set sail from Sicily.

Book VI marks a turning point in the poem, as Aeneas' uncertainty is transformed to resolution of purpose. He visits the Sibyl at Cumae; with the golden bough and guided by the Sibyl he goes down into the underworld to visit his father in the Elysian Fields. On his way through the different areas of Hades Aeneas meets Palinurus, his former helmsman, Dido and Deiphobus. There he also catches a glimpse of some of his former Greek enemies who flee from him in terror. On reaching the Elysian Fields he meets his father who shows him the great figures of future Roman history, waiting their turn to go up and take their place in the upper world. Fired by this vision of Rome's future greatness, Aeneas returns to press on with his mission.

In Book VII Aeneas at last enters Italy, the land of his destiny, by the river Tiber, thus fulfilling the prophecy of Creusa at the end of Book II. At first everything seems to be going well; Latinus, king of Latium, welcomes the Trojans since he sees Aeneas as a suitable husband for his daughter, Lavinia. However, Turnus, the prince of a neighbouring people, encouraged by Amata, Latinus' wife, considers that Lavinia was promised to him, and so he rouses up the Latins against the newcomers. War is declared and the book ends with a catalogue of the Italian forces; this is intended to remind the reader of the catalogue of the Greek ships in Book II of Homer's *Iliad*.

Book VIII describes how Aeneas prepares to face the might of the Latins. The river Tiber appears to him in a dream and tells him to go and seek help from Evander, a Greek who had settled on the site of the future city of Rome. Evander promises to send a detachment back with him under the leadership of his son, Pallas, and urges Aeneas to visit Tarchon, the Etruscan king, to raise more allies there. Evander then conducts Aeneas around the site of his city and explains the origins of some of the most ancient sites and customs of Rome as Virgil's audience knew them. Venus, ever concerned for her son's safety, persuades Vulcan, her husband, to make a new suit of armour for Aeneas; this again harks back to the shield which was made for Achilles in Book XVIII of Homer's *Iliad*. On Aeneas' shield are depicted various events in Roman history culminating in the battle of Actium, where Octavian, later to be the emperor Augustus, was victorious.

Aeneas plays no part in Book IX since it describes the events which take place at the Trojan camp in his absence. Turnus mounts two attacks on the camp. In the first he fails to storm it but sets the ships on fire. Two young Trojans, Nisus and Euryalus, try to slip through the Latin lines to inform Aeneas of the dangerous situation; though they kill a few of the enemy their mission fails with their own deaths. Next day Turnus and his Latin forces return to the attack and succeed in gaining a foothold inside the Trojan camp. However, Turnus is cut off and forced to escape by leaping into the river Tiber.

Book X opens unexpectedly in Jupiter's palace on Olympus. The bitter feuding there mirrors the fighting on earth; Venus and Juno engage in bitter recriminations which are silenced when Jupiter issues an edict. The story then returns to the plight of the Trojan camp; very soon, however, Aeneas appears sailing at the head of reinforcements. He raises his divine shield to signal his arrival and the beleaguered Trojans shout with relief. The next episode in the book concerns the fighting on the shore and concentrates on Pallas, the son of Evander. His Arcadian forces are thrown into disarray but Pallas raises their fighting spirit by rushing into the fray himself and killing a number of the enemy. As the battle rages, Turnus makes his entry and demands to face Pallas in single combat. In the duel Pallas grazes Turnus, but Turnus then fatally wounds Pallas with his spear and stands over him to boast in his moment of victory. With bitter words Turnus tears the belt from Pallas' body and thereby seals his own doom. The remainder of this book relates the fight between Aeneas and Mezentius, the Etruscan tyrant. At the moment when Aeneas is about to finish off his wounded opponent, Lausus, Mezentius' son, rushes to the rescue so that his father can withdraw from the battle and nurse his wound. Lausus is no match for Aeneas and quickly meets his death. With a touch of remorse Aeneas himself lifts the young man's body and hands it back to his comrades. Mezentius, weak from his wound and distraught at his son's death, mounts his horse with difficulty and rides back to inevitable death at the hands of Aeneas.

Book XI acts as an extended prelude to the final outcome of the story. The body of Pallas is taken home to Evander for burial and a twelve day truce is arranged for the burial of the dead on both sides. The Latins then hold a council of war at which various policies are proposed, with Turnus advocating a continuation of the war. As they debate, news arrives that the Trojans are on the move again and the war starts up afresh. A cavalry battle ensues with the Latin forces who are commanded by Camilla, a warrior princess. In the end Camilla is killed and the opposing armies encamp for the night.

The long-awaited clash between Aeneas and Turnus comes in Book XII and occupies virtually the entire book. Turnus realises that the morale of his forces is now broken and the only thing left is for him to meet Aeneas alone in single combat. Latinus and Amata vainly try to dissuade him. The confrontation, however, does not take place quickly; there is a slow build up of tension, with an elaborate description of Turnus arming himself. Then a setback occurs when the Rutulians break the truce and indiscriminate fighting is renewed between both armies. Eventually Turnus and Aeneas meet, and in an episode reminiscent of Achilles' fight with Hector in the *Iliad*, Aeneas wounds Turnus in the thigh. As he is about to relent and grant Turnus his life, he notices on Turnus the belt stripped from the body of Pallas; in a moment of blind rage Aeneas kills Turnus.

So the poem ends on a jarring note which many scholars in both ancient and more modern times have found disconcerting.

Virgil and his Predecessors

In various fields of literature the Romans looked to the works of earlier Greek writers as their models. The Homeric poems were such masterpieces of epic poetry that all succeeding writers, both Greek and Roman, felt obliged to acknowledge the inspiration they provided by re-using incidents and ideas taken from the *Iliad* and the *Odyssey*.

In the *Aeneid* we find strong echoes of the Homeric poems. In structure the early part of the *Aeneid* mirrors that of the *Odyssey*, with Aeneas recounting his adventures for Dido just as Odysseus does for Alcinous. Secondly, an important element in the final books of the *Aeneid* is the vengeful anger Aeneas harbours towards Turnus as a result of the death of his young friend and ally, Pallas. This is undoubtedly based on the consuming anger Achilles has for Hector in the *Iliad* because of the death of his friend Patroclus. Other parallels come easily to mind. Both heroes, Odysseus and Aeneas, visit the underworld, though the land of the dead is viewed quite differently in the two poems. There are funeral games, described in great detail, for Patroclus in the *Iliad* and for Anchises in the *Aeneid*. Two heroes, Achilles and Aeneas, are presented with new suits of armour by their mothers. In Book II of the *Iliad* there is a long catalogue of the various contingents of Greeks who constituted the besieging army at Troy. At the end of the seventh book of the *Aeneid* there is a similar catalogue, but this time of the Italian contingents that massed to oppose the Trojans. The world of the Homeric poems is peopled by heroes, impetuous individuals whose sole aim in life is to gain glory; this is done chiefly through exploits in war. The common people are shadowy participants, serving either as nameless victims in battle or subjects over whom the heroes exercise their sway. Social obligations hardly exist in Homeric society; concern for another person is only possible in the case of someone of equal status. In Virgil's *Aeneid*, however, we enter a different world. As a hero, Aeneas disregards his own feelings and wishes to a large extent and demonstrates a compassionate concern for his family and the people under his care. Furthermore, Aeneas is conscious of his obligations to the gods and the future of his race to a much greater degree than any Homeric hero and, for this, he is often described by the poet as 'pius'. His *pietas* is most graphically portrayed in the closing scene of Book II where he carries his father and the penates off into exile.

The poet or poets of the Homeric poems are constantly looking backwards to a lost age of martial glory and power; in contrast the *Aeneid* looks forward on two levels. Firstly, Aeneas spends little time and effort lamenting the past glories of Troy but concentrates his thoughts and words on the future. The main warfare section of the *Aeneid* – Virgil's *Iliad* – is set significantly at the site of Troy's successor, whereas the fighting in the *Iliad* marks the end of an era and has as its object the restoration of a hero's honour. On the second level Virgil, through his description of a heroic past, was pointing the way forward to a new Rome after the destruction of the recent civil war.

Links between the *Aeneid* and the Homeric poems abound and are certain, but it is much more difficult to gauge whether Virgil drew on ideas from other Greek authors. For example, does Dido in Book IV of the *Aeneid* owe anything to Medea in the *Argonautica* of Apollonius Rhodius? There is little doubt, however, that Virgil's account of the Trojan wanderings after they left their ruined city follows very closely the route described in a work by Dionysius of Halicarnassus. It is impossible to tell whether Virgil owed anything to the Roman writers before him, as only scanty fragments remain of the hexameter *Annales* of Ennius and of Naevius' *Bellum Ponticum*, written in Saturnian metre.

The *Aeneid* and Rome

Virgil was writing the *Aeneid* at a time when the Roman world had recently emerged from a period of civil war. Many people's lives had been shattered, the old republican system of government had been swept away and Augustus had established himself as supreme ruler of the Roman Empire. There was a wide-spread longing for peace and an end to lawlessness; most people wished to return to the traditional Roman values which had made Rome great, even if the political institutions associated with them had gone for ever. The poet Horace, Virgil's contemporary, lamented the deserted and derelict state of many shrines which symbolised for him the moral bankruptcy of contemporary Roman society (*Odes* III 6). In response to this feeling Augustus, when he came to power, introduced not only political, but also social and religious measures to restore the shattered fabric of society. In the *Aeneid* Virgil provided some of the inspiration needed to rally the Roman people to a rebuilding of Rome's greatness.

Although Aeneas is nominally the hero of the poem, in many ways the real focus of attention is the future city – eventually to be Rome itself. For Aeneas it is the future home towards which he is leading his band of followers; for the poet it is a common inheritance of which the Romans of his day should feel justly proud. It is no accident that Virgil's story begins chronologically with the Trojan War, for this gave the Romans a claim to be as ancient as the Greeks and this, through Aeneas, provided them with divine ancestors. At the same time, in tune with the mood of Virgil's own day, the *Aeneid* portrays Aeneas, the archetypal Roman, leading a remnant shattered by war forward into the future under the guidance of the gods. Thus the *Aeneid* is a poetic version of Rome's earliest history and an inspiration for the renewing of her life under the Augustan reforms.

Among various references to Roman history, the most obvious is that concerning Dido and Carthage in Book IV. Carthage for the Romans was a city of fearful memories, a power which under the leadership of Hannibal came very close to destroying Rome. Virgil capitalises on this by projecting the foundation of Carthage back in time and making Dido an insidious threat to the future destiny of Rome. Another echo of more recent events occurs in Book II where Virgil describes Priam's headless body lying on the beach; this must have reminded his audience of the murder of Pompeius in Egypt. A number of other references are made in Book VI when Aeneas is visiting the Underworld to see his father, Anchises. In the timeless setting of the land of the dead Virgil is able to recall the heroes of the Roman people from the earliest period right up to Julius Caesar, Pompeius and Augustus himself. The poet describes how Aeneas was inspired by the sight of these Romans waiting to be born and no doubt Virgil hoped that his audience and readers also would be inspired in the same way.

Thirdly, in Book VIII Aeneas is presented by his mother, Venus, with a new suit of armour forged and decorated by Vulcan. On the shield various scenes from future Roman history were depicted, with pride of place given to the battle of Actium and to Augustus. Also in Book VIII Evander, Aeneas' host, conducts Aeneas around the future site of the city of Rome pointing out features like the Tarpeian Rock and the Capitol, all very familiar to the Romans of Virgil's own day.

All these allusions serve the purpose of making the story thoroughly Roman in flavour as well as in language, and they bind a legend which was essentially one of prehistory to the stream of real Roman history. This gives the poem a reality and power which the simple story of a wandering hero could never have possessed, and transforms Aeneas into a true Roman of whom those of Virgil's day could justly feel proud.

SELECT BIBLIOGRAPHY

This bibliography is divided into two sections: **A** is regarded as suitable for readers preparing for GCSE examinations at 15+ ; **B** is for older students.

Section A

Anderson, W.S., *The Art of the Aeneid* (Bristol Classical Press, 1989).

Camps, W.A., *An Introduction to Virgil's Aeneid* (Oxford University Press, 1969).

Griffin, Jasper, *Virgil* (Oxford University Press, 1986; Past Masters).

Jenkyns, Richard, *Classical Epic, Homer and Virgil* (Bristol Classical Press, 1992; Classical World series).

Willams, R.D., *Aeneas and the Roman Hero* (Macmillan, 1973; Inside the Ancient World series).

Also the following issues of *Omnibus* (JACT) contain articles on Book II of the *Aeneid*:

Issue 16, P. Haney, *Aeneas and Sinon*;

Issue 18, G. Nussbaum, *Vergil's Fall of Troy*;

Issue 25, R. Jenkyns, *Virgil's Women*;

Issue 27, S. Harrison, *Aeneas at the fall of Troy*.

Section B

Cairns, F., *Virgil's Augustan Epic* (Cambridge University Press, 1989).

Commager, Steele (ed.), *Virgil, a Collection of Critical Essays*, 20th Century Views (Prentice-Hall, 1966). See especially B. Knox, *The Serpent and the Flame*.

Gransden, K.W., *Virgil's Iliad* (Cambridge University Press, 1984).

Hunt, J.W., *Forms of Glory* (South Illinois University Press, 1973).

Lyne, R.O.A.M., *Further Voices in Vergil's Aeneid* (Oxford University Press, 1987).

Otis, Brooks, *Virgil, a Study in Civilized Poetry* (Oxford University Press, 1963).

Quinn, K., *Virgil's Aeneid, a Critical Description* (Routledge & Kegan Paul, 1968).

Williams, G., *Technique and Ideas in the Aeneid* (Yale, 1983).

Williams, R.D., *The Aeneid* (Allen and Unwin, 1987).

AENEID BOOK II

*Aeneas asked by Dido to describe the destruction of Troy
and the wanderings of the Trojans reluctantly begins.*

Conticuere omnes intentique ora tenebant.
inde toro pater Aeneas sic orsus ab alto:
'infandum, regina, iubes renovare dolorem,
Troianas ut opes et lamentabile regnum
5   eruerint Danai, quaeque ipse miserrima vidi
et quorum pars magna fui. quis talia fando
Myrmidonum Dolopumve aut duri miles Vlixi
temperet a lacrimis? et iam nox umida caelo
praecipitat suadentque cadentia sidera somnos.
10   sed si tantus amor casus cognoscere nostros
et breviter Troiae supremum audire laborem,
quamquam animus meminisse horret luctuque refugit,
incipiam.

*The demoralised Greeks build a wooden horse,
fill it with men and depart leaving it on the shore.*

Fracti bello fatisque repulsi
ductores Danaum tot iam labentibus annis
15   instar montis equum divina Palladis arte
aedificant, sectaque intexunt abiete costas;
votum pro reditu simulant; ea fama vagatur.
huc delecta virum sortiti corpora furtim
includunt caeco lateri penitusque cavernas
20   ingentes uterumque armato milite complent.
est in conspectu Tenedos, notissima fama
insula, dives opum Priami dum regna manebant,
nunc tantum sinus et statio male fida carinis:
huc se provecti deserto in litore condunt.

*The Trojans discuss what to do with the horse;
Laocoon warns that it is a Greek trick.*

25   Nos abiisse rati et vento petiisse Mycenas.
ergo omnis longo solvit se Teucria luctu:
panduntur portae, iuvat ire et Dorica castra
desertosque videre locos litusque relictum:

hic Dolopum manus, hic saevus tendebat Achilles;
30   classibus hic locus, hic acie certare solebant.
pars stupet innuptae donum exitiale Minervae
et molem mirantur equi; primusque Thymoetes
duci intra muros hortatur et arce locari,
sive dolo seu iam Troiae sic fata ferebant.
35   at Capys, et quorum melior sententia menti,
aut pelago Danaum insidias suspectaque dona
praecipitare iubent subiectisve urere flammis,
aut terebrare cavas uteri et temptare latebras.
scinditur incertum studia in contraria vulgus.
40   primus ibi ante omnes magna comitante caterva
Laocoon ardens summa decurrit ab arce,
et procul 'o miseri, quae tanta insania, cives?
creditis avectos hostes? aut ulla putatis
dona carere dolis Danaum? sic notus Vlixes?
45   aut hoc inclusi ligno occultantur Achivi,
aut haec in nostros fabricata est machina muros,
inspectura domos venturaque desuper urbi,
aut aliquis latet error; equo ne credite, Teucri.
quidquid id est, timeo Danaos et dona ferentes.'
50   sic fatus validis ingentem viribus hastam
in latus inque feri curvam compagibus alvum
contorsit. stetit illa tremens, uteroque recusso
insonuere cavae gemitumque dedere cavernae.
et, si fata deum, si mens non laeva fuisset,
55   impulerat ferro Argolicas foedare latebras,
Troiaque nunc staret, Priamique arx alta maneres.

A terrified Greek captive is brought by shepherds;
he is asked to explain the purpose of the horse.

Ecce, manus iuvenem interea post terga revinctum
pastores magno ad regem clamore trahebant
Dardanidae, qui se ignotum venientibus ultro,
60   hoc ipsum ut strueret Troiamque aperiret Achivis,
obtulerat, fidens animi atque in utrumque paratus,
seu versare dolos seu certae occumbere morti.
undique visendi studio Troiana iuventus
circumfusa ruit certantque inludere capto.
65   accipe nunc Danaum insidias et crimine ab uno

disce omnes.
namque ut conspectu in medio turbatus, inermis,
constitit atque oculis Phrygia agmina circumspexit:
'heu, quae me tellus' inquit 'quae me aequora possunt
70   accipere? aut quid iam misero mihi denique restat,
cui neque apud Danaos usquam locus, et super ipsi
Dardanidae infensi poenas cum sanguine poscunt?'
quo gemitu conversi animi compressus et omnis
impetus. hortamur fari quo sanguine cretus,
75   quidve ferat; memoret quae sit fiducia capto.
[ille haec deposita tandem formidine fatur:]

The prisoner, Sinon, begins by describing
his own quarrel with the Greek leader, Ulysses.

'Cuncta equidem tibi, rex, fuerit quodcumque, fatebor
vera,' inquit, 'neque me Argolica de gente negabo;
hoc primum; nec, si miserum fortuna Sinonem
80   finxit, vanum etiam mendacemque improba finget.
fando aliquod si forte tuas pervenit ad aures
Belidae nomen Palamedis et incluta fama
gloria, quem falsa sub proditione Pelasgi
insontem infando indicio, quia bella vetabat,
85   demisere neci, nunc cassum lumine lugent:
illi me comitem et consanguinitate propinquum
pauper in arma pater primis huc misit ab annis.
dum stabat regno incolumis regumque vigebat
conciliis, et nos aliquod nomenque decusque
90   gessimus. invidia postquam pellacis Vlixi
(haud ignota loquor) superis concessit ab oris,
adflictus vitam in tenebris luctuque trahebam
et casum insontis mecum indignabar amici.
nec tacui demens et me, fors si qua tulisset,
95   si patrios umquam remeassem victor ad Argos,
promisi ultorem et verbis odia aspera movi.
hinc mihi prima mali labes, hinc semper Vlixes
criminibus terrere novis, hinc spargere voces
in vulgum ambiguas et quaerere conscius arma.
100   nec requievit enim, donec Calchante ministro -
sed quid ego haec autem nequiquam ingrata revolvo,
quidve moror? si omnes uno ordine habetis Achivos,

3

idque audire sat est, iamdudum sumite poenas:
hoc Ithacus velit et magno mercentur Atridae.'

*The Trojans want to hear more. Sinon tells how the Greeks try to regain
the favour of the gods by human sacrifice and how he escaped.*

105   Tum vero ardemus scitari et quaerere causas,
ignari scelerum tantorum artisque Pelasgae.
prosequitur pavitans et ficto pectore fatur:
'saepe fugam Danai Troia cupiere relicta
moliri et longo fessi discedere bello;
110   fecissentque utinam! saepe illos aspera ponti
interclusit hiems et terruit Auster euntes.
praecipue cum iam hic trabibus contextus acernis
staret equus toto sonuerunt aethere nimbi.
suspensi Eurypylum scitantem oracula Phoebi
115   mittimus, isque adytis haec tristia dicta reportat:
"sanguine placastis ventos et virgine caesa,
cum primum Iliacas, Danai, venistis ad oras:
sanguine quaerendi reditus animaque litandum
Argolica." vulgi quae vox ut venit ad aures,
120   obstipuere animi gelidusque per ima cucurrit
ossa tremor, cui fata parent, quem poscat Apollo.
hic Ithacus vatem magno Calchanta tumultu
protrahit in medios; quae sint ea numina divum
flagitat. et mihi iam multi crudele canebant
125   artificis scelus, et taciti ventura videbant.
bis quinos silet ille dies tectusque recusat
prodere voce sua quemquam aut opponere morti.
vix tandem, magnis Ithaci clamoribus actus,
composito rumpit vocem et me destinat arae.
130   adsensere omnes et, quae sibi quisque timebat,
unius in miseri exitium conversa tulere.
iamque dies infanda aderat; mihi sacra parari
et salsae fruges et circum tempora vittae.
eripui, fateor, leto me et vincula rupi,
135   limosoque lacu per noctem obscurus in ulva
delitui dum vela darent, si forte dedissent.
nec mihi iam patriam antiquam spes ulla videndi,
nec dulces natos exoptatumque parentem,
quos illi fors et poenas ob nostra reposcent

140   effugia, et culpam hanc miserorum morte piabunt.
quod te per superos et conscia numina veri,
per si qua est quae restet adhuc mortalibus usquam
intemerata fides, oro, miserere laborum
tantorum, miserere animi non digna ferentis.'

Sinon's lies are believed. Priam frees Sinon from his bonds
and asks him to explain the purpose of the horse.

145   His lacrimis vitam damus et miserescimus ultro.
ipse viro primus manicas atque arta levari
vincla iubet Priamus dictisque ita fatur amicis:
'quisquis es (amissos hinc iam obliviscere Graios)
noster eris; mihique haec edissere vera roganti:
150   quo molem hanc immanis equi statuere? quis auctor?
quidve petunt? quae religio? aut quae machina belli?'
dixerat. ille dolis instructus et arte Pelasga
sustulit exutas vinclis ad sidera palmas:
'vos aeterni ignes, et non violabile vestrum
155   testor numen,' ait, 'vos arae ensesque nefandi,
quos fugi, vittaeque deum, quas hostia gessi:
fas mihi Graiorum sacrata resolvere iura,
fas odisse viros atque omnia ferre sub auras,
si qua tegunt; teneor patriae nec legibus ullis.
160   tu modo promissis maneas servataque serves
Troia fidem, si vera feram, si magna rependam.

Sinon describes how the Greeks angered Pallas and were told to seek
the favour of the gods again. The horse was left as a gift to Pallas,
deliberately built so large that it could not be taken inside the city.

     Omnis spes Danaum et coepti fiducia belli
Palladis auxiliis semper stetit. impius ex quo
Tydides sed enim scelerumque inventor Vlixes
165   fatale adgressi sacrato avellere templo
Palladium caesis summae custodibus arcis
corripuere sacram effigiem manibusque cruentis
virgineas ausi divae contingere vittas:
ex illo fluere ac retro sublapsa referri
170   spes Danaum, fractae vires, aversa deae mens.
nec dubiis ea signa dedit Tritonia monstris.
vix positum castris simulacrum: arsere coruscae

luminibus flammae arrectis, salsusque per artus
sudor iit, terque ipsa solo (mirabile dictu)
175 emicuit parmamque ferens hastamque trementem.
extemplo temptanda fuga canit aequora Calchas,
nec posse Argolicis exscindi Pergama telis
omina ni repetant Argis numenque reducant
quod pelago et curvis secum avexere carinis.
180 et nunc quod patrias vento petiere Mycenas,
arma deosque parant comites pelagoque remenso
improvisi aderunt. ita digerit omina Calchas.
hanc pro Palladio moniti, pro numine laeso
effigiem statuere, nefas quae triste piaret.
185 hanc tamen immensam Calchas attollere molem
roboribus textis caeloque educere iussit,
ne recipi portis aut duci in moenia posset,
neu populum antiqua sub religione tueri.
nam si vestra manus violasset dona Minervae,
190 tum magnum exitium (quod di prius omen in ipsum
convertant!) Priami imperio Phrygibusque futurum;
sin manibus vestris vestram ascendisset in urbem,
ultro Asiam magno Pelopea ad moenia bello
venturam et nostros ea fata manere nepotes.'

*Again Sinon is believed. Laocoon and his sons
are killed by two snakes sent by Pallas.*

195 Talibus insidiis periurique arte Sinonis
credita res, captique dolis lacrimisque coactis
quos neque Tydides nec Larissaeus Achilles,
non anni domuere decem, non mille carinae.
hic aliud maius miseris multoque tremendum
200 obicitur magis atque improvida pectora turbat.
Laocoon, ductus Neptuno sorte sacerdos,
sollemnes taurum ingentem mactabat ad aras.
ecce autem gemini a Tenedo tranquilla per alta
(horresco referens) immensis orbibus angues
205 incumbunt pelago pariterque ad litora tendunt;
pectora quorum inter fluctus arrecta iubaeque
sanguineae superant undas; pars cetera pontum
pone legit sinuatque immensa volumine terga.
fit sonitus spumante salo; iamque arva tenebant

'ILLE SIMUL MANIBUS TENDIT DIVELLERE NODOS'

The serpents destroy Laocoon and his sons.
(Marble group in the Vatican.)

210 ardentesque oculos suffecti sanguine et igni
sibila lambebant linguis vibrantibus ora.
diffugimus visu exsangues. illi agmine certo
Laocoonta petunt; et primum parva duorum
corpora natorum serpens amplexus uterque
215 implicat et miseros morsu depascitur artus;
post ipsum auxilio subeuntem ac tela ferentem
corripiunt spirisque ligant ingentibus; et iam
bis medium amplexi, bis collo squamea circum
terga dati superant capite et cervicibus altis.
220 ille simul manibus tendit divellere nodos
perfusus sanie vittas atroque veneno,
clamores simul horrendos ad sidera tollit:
qualis mugitus, fugit cum saucius aram
taurus et incertam excussit cervice securim.
225 at gemini lapsu delubra ad summa dracones
effugiunt saevaeque petunt Tritonidis arcem,
sub pedibusque deae clipeique sub orbe teguntur.

The fate of Laocoon is taken as an omen;
the Trojans open their walls and bring the horse inside.

Tum vero tremefacta novus per pectora cunctis
insinuat pavor, et scelus expendisse merentem
230 Laocoonta ferunt, sacrum qui cuspide robur
laeserit et tergo sceleratam intorserit hastam.
ducendum ad sedes simulacrum orandaque divae
numina conclamant.
dividimus muros et moenia pandimus urbis.
235 accingunt omnes operi pedibusque rotarum
subiciunt lapsus, et stuppea vincula collo
intendunt: scandit fatalis machina muros
feta armis. pueri circum innuptaeque puellae
sacra canunt funemque manu contingere gaudent:
240 illa subit mediaeque minans inlabitur urbi.
o patria, o divum domus Ilium et incluta bello
moenia Dardanidum! quater ipso in limine portae
substitit atque utero sonitum quater arma dedere;
instamus tamen immemores caecique furore
245 et monstrum infelix sacrata sistimus arce.
tunc etiam fatis aperit Cassandra futuris

ora dei iussu non umquam credita Teucris.
nos delubra deum miseri, quibus ultimus esset
ille dies, festa velamus fronde per urbem.

*While the Trojans sleep, the Greeks return
and Sinon releases the men from the horse.*

250   Vertitur interea caelum et ruit Oceano nox
involvens umbra magna terramque polumque
Myrmidonumque dolos; fusi per moenia Teucri
conticuere; sopor fessos complectitur artus.
et iam Argiva phalanx instructis navibus ibat
255   a Tenedo tacitae per amica silentia lunae
litora nota petens, flammas cum regia puppis
extulerat, fatisque deum defensus iniquis
inclusos utero Danaos et pinea furtim
laxat claustra Sinon. illos patefactus ad auras
260   reddit equus, laetique cavo se robore promunt
Thessandrus Sthenelusque duces et dirus Vlixes,
demissum lapsi per funem, Acamasque Thoasque
Pelidesque Neoptolemus primusque Machaon
et Menelaus et ipse doli fabricator Epeos.
265   invadunt urbem somno vinoque sepultam;
caeduntur vigiles, portisque patentibus omnes
accipiunt socios atque agmina conscia iungunt.

*The ghost of Hector appears to Aeneas
and urges him to leave the doomed city.*

Tempus erat quo prima quies mortalibus aegris
incipit et dono divum gratissima serpit.
270   in somnis, ecce, ante oculos maestissimus Hector
. visus adesse mihi largosque effundere fletus,
raptatus bigis ut quondam, aterque cruento
pulvere perque pedes traiectus lora tumentes.
ei mihi, qualis erat, quantum mutatus ab illo
275   Hectore qui redit exuvias indutus Achilli,
vel Danaum Phrygios iaculatus puppibus ignes;
squalentem barbam et concretos sanguine crines
vulneraque illa gerens, quae circum plurima muros
accepit patrios. ultro flens ipse videbar
280   compellare virum et maestas expromere voces:

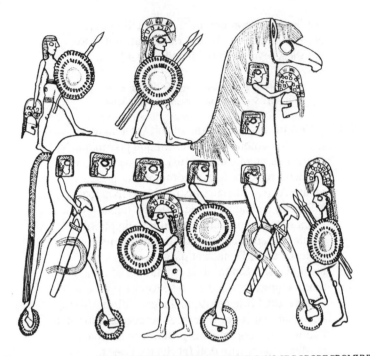

'Illos patefactus ad auras reddit equus, laetique cavo se robore promunt'

Trojan Horse
(From Greek relief vase of 7th century BC, Mykonos.)

Hector's Body Dragged Behind the Chariot of Achilles

The winged figure is the ghost of Hector's victim Partoclus; the charioteer is Automedon, and Achilles, helmeted, is seen behind the horses.
(From a Greek vase c.500 BC.)

10

'o lux Dardaniae, spes o fidissima Teucrum,
quae tantae tenuere morae? quibus, Hector, ab oris
exspectate venis? ut te post multa tuorum
funera, post varios hominumque urbisque labores
285   defessi aspicimus! quae causa indigna serenos
foedavit vultus? aut cur haec vulnera cerno?'
ille nihil, nec me quaerentem vana moratur,
sed graviter gemitus imo de pectore ducens,
'heu fuge, nate dea, teque his' ait 'eripe flammis.
290   hostis habet muros; ruit alto a culmine Troia.
sat patriae Priamoque datum: si Pergama dextra
defendi possent, etiam hac defensa fuissent.
sacra suosque tibi commendat Troia penates;
hos cape fatorum comites, his moenia quaere,
295   magna pererrato statues quae denique ponto.'
sic ait et manibus vittas Vestamque potentem
aeternumque adytis effert penetralibus ignem.

Aeneas wakens to find the city in flames;
he grabs his armour and goes out to fight.

Diverso interea miscentur moenia luctu,
et magis atque magis, quamquam secreta parentis
300   Anchisae domus arboribusque obtecta recessit,
clarescunt sonitus armorumque ingruit horror.
excutior somno et summi fastigia tecti
ascensu supero atque arrectis auribus asto:
in segetem veluti cum flamma furentibus Austris
305   incidit, aut rapidus montano flumine torrens
sternit agros, sternit sata laeta boumque labores
praecipitesque trahit silvas: stupet inscius alto
accipiens sonitum saxi de vertice pastor.
tum vero manifesta fides, Danaumque patescunt
310   insidiae. iam Deiphobi dedit ampla ruinam
Volcano superante domus, iam proximus ardet
Ucalegon; Sigea igni freta lata relucent.
exoritur clamorque virum clangorque tubarum.
arma amens capio; nec sat rationis in armis,
315   sed glomerare manum bello et concurrere in arcem
cum sociis ardent animi; furor iraque mentem
praecipitat, pulchrumque mori succurrit in armis.

11

Virgil: Aeneid II

*Aeneas meets Panthus, the priest of Apollo,
who tells him that the Greeks control the city.*

　　Ecce autem telis Panthus elapsus Achivum,
　　Panthus Othryades, arcis Phoebique sacerdos,
320　sacra manu victosque deos parvumque nepotem
　　ipse trahit cursuque amens ad limina tendit.
　　'quo res summa loco, Panthu? quam prendimus arcem?'
　　vix ea fatus eram gemitu cum talia reddit:
　　'venit summa dies et ineluctabile tempus
325　Dardaniae. fuimus Troes, fuit Ilium et ingens
　　gloria Teucrorum; ferus omnia Iuppiter Argos
　　transtulit, incensa Danai dominantur in urbe.
　　arduus armatos mediis in moenibus astans
　　fundit equus victorque Sinon incendia miscet
330　insultans. portis alii bipatentibus adsunt,
　　milia quot magnis umquam venere Mycenis;
　　obsedere alii telis angusta viarum
　　oppositis; stat ferri acies mucrone corusco
　　stricta, parata neci; vix primi proelia temptant
335　portarum vigiles et caeco Marte resistunt.'

*Aeneas collects a band of Trojans
and they prepare to resist as best they can.*

　　Talibus Othryadae dictis et numine divum
　　in flammas et in arma feror, quo tristis Erinys
　　quo fremitus vocat et sublatus ad aethera clamor.
　　addunt se socios Rhipeus et maximus armis
340　Epytus, oblati per lunam, Hypanisque Dymasque
　　et lateri adglomerant nostro, iuvenisque Coroebus
　　Mygdonides - illis ad Troiam forte diebus
　　venerat insano Cassandrae incensus amore
　　et gener auxilium Priamo Phrygibusque ferebat,
345　infelix qui non sponsae praecepta furentis
　　audierit!
　　quos ubi confertos audere in proelia vidi,
　　incipio super his: 'iuvenes, fortissima frustra
　　pectora, si vobis audendi extrema cupido
350　certa sequi, quae sit rebus fortuna videtis;
　　excessere omnes adytis arisque relictis
　　di quibus imperium hoc steterat; succurritis urbi

12

incensae: moriamur et in media arma ruamus.
una salus victis nullam sperare salutem.'
355   sic animis iuvenum furor additus. inde, lupi ceu
raptores atra in nebula, quos improba ventris
exegit caecos rabies catulique relicti
faucibus exspectant siccis, per tela, per hostes
vadimus haud dubiam in mortem mediaeque tenemus
360   urbis iter; nox atra cava circumvolat umbra.
quis cladem illius noctis, quis funera fando
explicet aut possit lacrimis aequare labores?
urbs antiqua ruit multos dominata per annos;
plurima perque vias sternuntur inertia passim
365   corpora perque domos et religiosa deorum
limina. nec soli poenas dant sanguine Teucri;
quondam etiam victis redit in praecordia virtus
victoresque cadunt Danai. crudelis ubique
luctus, ubique pavor et plurima mortis imago.

Aeneas and his band overwhelm some Greeks and take their armour;
with this disguise they gain some successes.

370   Primus se Danaum magna comitante caterva
Androgeos offert nobis, socia agmina credens
inscius, atque ultro verbis compellat amicis:
'festinate, viri! nam quae tam sera moratur
segnities? alii rapiunt incensa feruntque
375   Pergama: vos celsis nunc primum a navibus itis?'
dixit, et extemplo (neque enim responsa dabantur
fida satis) sensit medios delapsus in hostes.
obstipuit retroque pedem cum voce repressit.
improvisum aspris veluti qui sentibus anguem
380   pressit humi nitens trepidusque repente refugit
attollentem iras et caerula colla tumentem,
haud secus Androgeos visu tremefactus abibat.
inruimus densis et circumfundimur armis,
ignarosque loci passim et formidine captos
385   sternimus. aspirat primo Fortuna labori.
atque hic successu exsultans animisque Coroebus
'o socii, qua prima' inquit 'fortuna salutis
monstrat iter, quaque ostendit se dextra, sequamur:
mutemus clipeos Danaumque insignia nobis

13

390 aptemus. dolus an virtus, quis in hoste requirat?
arma dabunt ipsi.' sic fatus deinde comantem
Androgeo galeam clipeique insigne decorum
induitur laterique Argivum accommodat ensem.
hoc Rhipeus, hoc ipse Dymas omnisque iuventus
395 laeta facit: spoliis se quisque recentibus armat.
vadimus immixti Danais haud numine nostro
multaque per caecam congressi proelia noctem
conserimus, multos Danaum demittimus Orco.
diffugiunt alii ad naves et litora cursu
400 fida petunt; pars ingentem formidine turpi
scandunt rursus equum et nota conduntur in alvo.

*Coroebus attempts to rescue the captured Cassandra; the Greeks resist
and Aeneas' men find themselves also attacked by fellow Trojans.*

Heu nihil invitis fas quemquam fidere divis!
ecce trahebatur passis Priameia virgo
crinibus a templo Cassandra adytisque Minervae
405 ad caelum tendens ardentia lumina frustra,
lumina, nam teneras arcebant vincula palmas.
non tulit hanc speciem furiata mente Coroebus
et sese medium iniecit periturus in agmen.
consequimur cuncti et densis incurrimus armis.
410 hic primum ex alto delubri culmine telis
nostrorum obruimur oriturque miserrima caedes
armorum facie et Graiarum errore iubarum.
tum Danai gemitu atque ereptae virginis ira
undique collecti invadunt, acerrimus Aiax
415 et gemini Atridae Dolopumque exercitus omnis;
adversi rupto ceu quondam turbine venti
confligunt, Zephyrusque Notusque et laetus Eois
Eurus equis; stridunt silvae saevitque tridenti
spumeus atque imo Nereus ciet aequora fundo.
420 illi etiam, si quos obscura nocte per umbram
fudimus insidiis totaque agitavimus urbe,
apparent; primi clipeos mentitaque tela
agnoscunt atque ora sono discordia signant.
ilicet obruimur numero; primusque Coroebus
425 Penelei dextra divae armipotentis ad aram
procumbit; cadit et Rhipeus, iustissimus unus

qui fuit in Teucris et servantissimus aequi
(dis aliter visum); pereunt Hypanisque Dymasque
confixi a sociis; nec te tua plurima, Panthu,
430 labentem pietas nec Apollinis infula texit.
Iliaci cineres et flamma extrema meorum,
testor, in occasu vestro nec tela nec ullas
vitavisse vices Danaum et, si fata fuissent
ut caderem, meruisse manu. divellimur inde,
435 Iphitus et Pelias mecum (quorum Iphitus aevo
iam gravior, Pelias et vulnere tardus Vlixi),
protinus ad sedes Priami clamore vocati.

Aeneas and a few others find a battle raging around Priam's palace;
they enter at the back and help to defend it from the roof.

Hic vero ingentem pugnam, ceu cetera nusquam
bella forent, nulli tota morerentur in urbe,
440 sic Martem indomitum Danaosque ad tecta ruentes
cernimus obsessumque acta testudine limen.
haerent parietibus scalae postesque sub ipsos
nituntur gradibus clipeosque ad tela sinistris
protecti obiciunt, prensant fastigia dextris.
445 Dardanidae contra turres ac tota domorum
culmina convellunt; his se, quando ultima cernunt,
extrema iam in morte parant defendere telis;
aurataceque trabes, veterum decora alta parentum,
devolvunt; alii strictis mucronibus imas
450 obsedere fores, has servant agmine denso.
instaurati animi regis succurrere tectis
auxilioque levare viros vimque addere victis.
limen erat caecaeque fores et pervius usus
tectorum inter se Priami, postesque relicti
455 a tergo, infelix qua se, dum regna manebant,
saepius Andromache ferre incomitata solebat
ad soceros et avo puerum Astyanacta trahebat.
evado ad summi fastigia culminis, unde
tela manu miseri iactabant inrita Teucri.
460 turrim in praecipiti stantem summisque sub astra
eductam tectis, unde omnis Troia videri
et Danaum solitae naves et Achaica castra,
adgressi ferro circum, qua summa labantes

ANDROMACHE, HOLDING HER CHILD ASTYANAX, AND HER HUSBAND HECTOR
(From a vase of the 5th century BC, in the British Museum.)

iuncturas tabulata dabant, convellimus altis
465   sedibus impulimusque; ea lapsa repente ruinam
cum sonitu trahit et Danaum super agmina late
incidit. ast alii subeunt, nec saxa nec ullum
telorum interea cessat genus.

Pyrrhus at the head of a band of Greeks smashes his way into the palace.

    Vestibulum ante ipsum primoque in limine Pyrrhus
470   exsultat telis et luce coruscus aena;
qualis ubi in lucem coluber mala gramina pastus,
frigida sub terra tumidum quem bruma tegebat,
nunc, positis novus exuviis nitidusque iuventa,
lubrica convolvit sublato pectore terga
475   arduus ad solem, et linguis micat ore trisulcis.
una ingens Periphas et equorum agitator Achillis,
armiger Automedon, una omnis Scyria pubes
succedunt tecto et flammas ad culmina iactant.
ipse inter primos correpta dura bipenni
480   limina perrumpit postesque a cardine vellit
aeratos; iamque excisa trabe firma cavavit
robora et ingentem lato dedit ore fenestram.
apparet domus intus et atria longa patescunt;
apparent Priami et veterum penetralia regum,
485   armatosque vident stantes in limine primo.
at domus interior gemitu miseroque tumultu
miscetur, penitusque cavae plangoribus aedes
femineis ululant; ferit aurea sidera clamor.
tum pavidae tectis matres ingentibus errant
490   amplexaeque tenent postes atque oscula figunt.
instat vi patria Pyrrhus; nec claustra nec ipsi
custodes sufferre valent; labat ariete crebro
ianua, et emoti procumbunt cardine postes.
fit via vi; rumpunt aditus primosque trucidant
495   immissi Danai et late loca milite complent.
non sic aggeribus ruptis cum spumeus amnis
exiit oppositasque evicit gurgite moles,
fertur in arva furens cumulo camposque per omnes
cum stabulis armenta trahit. vidi ipse furentem
500   caede Neoptolemum geminosque in limine Atridas,
vidi Hecubam centumque nurus Priamumque per aras

sanguine foedantem quos ipse sacraverat ignes.
quinquaginta illi thalami, spes ampla nepotum,
barbarico postes auro spoliisque superbi
505 procubuere; tenent Danai qua deficit ignis.

*The aged Priam prepares to resist, but is persuaded
by Hecuba, his wife, to take refuge at the altar.*

Forsitan et Priami fuerint quae fata requiras.
urbis uti captae casum convulsaque vidit
limina tectorum et medium in penetralibus hostem,
arma diu senior desueta trementibus aevo
510 circumdat nequiquam umeris et inutile ferrum
cingitur, ac densos fertur moriturus in hostes.
aedibus in mediis nudoque sub aetheris axe
ingens ara fuit iuxtaque veterrima laurus
incumbens arae atque umbra complexa penates.
515 hic Hecuba et natae nequiquam altaria circum,
praecipites atra ceu tempestate columbae,
condensae et divum amplexae simulacra sedebant.
ipsum autem sumptis Priamum iuvenalibus armis
ut vidit, 'quae mens tam dira, miserrime coniunx,
520 impulit his cingi telis? aut quo ruis?' inquit.
'non tali auxilio nec defensoribus istis
tempus eget; non, si ipse meus nunc adforet Hector.
huc tandem concede; haec ara tuebitur omnes,
aut moriere simul.' sic ore effata recepit
525 ad sese et sacra longaevum in sede locavit.

*Polites, Priam's son, is pursued and killed by Pyrrhus;
Priam seeks for vengeance and is also killed.*

Ecce autem elapsus Pyrrhi de caede Polites,
unus natorum Priami, per tela, per hostes
porticibus longis fugit et vacua atria lustrat
saucius. illum ardens infesto vulnere Pyrrhus
530 insequitur, iam iamque manu tenet et premit hasta.
ut tandem ante oculos evasit et ora parentum,
concidit ac multo vitam cum sanguine fudit.
hic Priamus, quamquam in media iam morte tenetur,
non tamen abstinuit nec voci iraeque pepercit:
535 'at tibi pro scelere,' exclamat, 'pro talibus ausis
18

'HAEC FINIS PRIAMI FATORUM'

Pyrrhus with Polites and Priam, Menelaus and Helen (left), Hecuba (right) and Hector's body below altar.
(From Athenian vase of 6th century BC, Berlin.)

di, si qua est caelo pietas quae talia curet,
persolvant grates dignas et praemia reddant
debita, qui nati coram me cernere letum
fecisti et patrios foedasti funere vultus.
540 at non ille, satum quo te mentiris, Achilles
talis in hoste fuit Priamo; sed iura fidemque
supplicis erubuit corpusque exsangue sepulcro
reddidit Hectoreum meque in mea regna remisit.'
sic fatus senior telumque imbelle sine ictu
545 coniecit, rauco quod protinus aere repulsum,
et summo clipei nequiquam umbone pependit.
cui Pyrrhus: 'referes ergo haec et nuntius ibis
Pelidae genitori. illi mea tristia facta
degeneremque Neoptolemum narrare memento.
550 nunc morere.' hoc dicens altaria ad ipsa trementem
traxit et in multo lapsantem sanguine nati,
implicuitque comam laeva, dextraque coruscum
extulit ac lateri capulo tenus abdidit ensem.
haec finis Priami fatorum, hic exitus illum
555 sorte tulit Troiam incensam et prolapsa videntem
Pergama, tot quondam populis terrisque superbum
regnatorem Asiae. iacet ingens litore truncus,
avulsumque umeris caput et sine nomine corpus.

Aeneas is reminded of his own family;
he catches sight of Helen and debates whether he should kill her.

At me tum primum saevus circumstetit horror.
560 obstipui; subiit cari genitoris imago,
ut regem aequaevum crudeli vulnere vidi
vitam exhalantem; subiit deserta Creusa
et direpta domus et parvi casus Iuli.
respicio et quae sit me circum copia lustro.
565 deseruere omnes defessi, et corpora saltu
ad terram misere aut ignibus aegra dedere.
iamque adeo super unus eram, cum limina Vestae
servantem et tacitam secreta in sede latentem
Tyndarida aspicio; dant clara incendia lucem
570 erranti passimque oculos per cuncta ferenti.
illa sibi infestos eversa ob Pergama Teucros
et poenas Danaum et deserti coniugis iras

ITALIAN 15TH-CENTURY MANUSCRIPT

With a margin addition of lines 567-588 of *Aeneid II*, in which Aeneas almost kills Helen when he meets her in Troy. On Virgil's instructions, this passage was deleted from the poem after his death. (Harley MS 2472 f.19b; British Library.)

Virgil: Aeneid II

PAPYRUS FRAGMENT OF A ROMAN WRITING EXERCISE,

1st century AD, which repeats line 601 of *Aeneid II*.

praemetuens, Troiae et patriae communis Erinys,
abdiderat sese atque aris invisa sedebat.
575 exarsere ignes animo; subit ira cadentem
ulcisci patriam et sceleratas sumere poenas.
'scilicet haec Spartam incolumis patriasque Mycenas
aspiciet, partoque ibit regina triumpho,
coniugiumque domumque patris natosque videbit
580 Iliadum turba et Phrygiis comitata ministris?
occiderit ferro Priamus? Troia arserit igni?
Dardanium totiens sudarit sanguine litus?
non ita. namque etsi nullum memorabile nomen
feminea in poena est nec habet victoria laudem,
585 exstinxisse nefas tamen et sumpsisse merentes
laudabor poenas, animumque explesse iuvabit
ultricis flammae et cineres satiasse meorum.'

Venus appears to Aeneas and tells him to defend his family;
she shows him how the great gods are also destroying the city.

Talia iactabam et furiata mente ferebar,
cum mihi se, non ante oculis tam clara, videndam
590 obtulit et pura per noctem in luce refulsit
alma parens, confessa deam qualisque videri
caelicolis et quanta solet, dextraque prehensum
continuit roseoque haec insuper addidit ore:
'nate, quis indomitas tantus dolor excitat iras?
595 quid furis aut quonam nostri tibi cura recessit?
non prius aspicies ubi fessum aetate parentem
liqueris Anchisen, superet coniunxne Creusa
Ascaniusque puer? quos omnes undique Graiae
circum errant acies et, ni mea cura resistat,
600 iam flammae tulerint inimicus et hauserit ensis.
non tibi Tyndaridis facies invisa Lacaenae
culpatusve Paris, divum inclementia, divum,
has evertit opes sternitque a culmine Troiam.
aspice (namque omnem, quae nunc obducta tuenti
605 mortales hebetat visus tibi et umida circum
caligat, nubem eripiam; tu ne qua parentis
iussa time neu praeceptis parere recusa):
hic, ubi disiectas moles avulsaque saxis
saxa vides, mixtoque undantem pulvere fumum,

610 Neptunus muros magnoque emota tridenti
fundamenta quatit totamque a sedibus urbem
eruit. hic Iuno Scaeas saevissima portas
prima tenet sociumque furens a navibus agmen
ferro accincta vocat.
615 iam summas arces Tritonia, respice, Pallas
insedit nimbo effulgens et Gorgone saeva.
ipse pater Danais animos viresque secundas
sufficit, ipse deos in Dardana suscitat arma.
eripe, nate, fugam finemque impone labori.
620 nusquam abero et tutum patrio te limine sistam.'
dixerat et spissis noctis se condidit umbris.
apparent dirae facies inimicaque Troiae
numina magna deum.
tum vero omne mihi visum considere in ignes
625 Ilium et ex imo verti Neptunia Troia;
ac veluti summis antiquam in montibus ornum
cum ferro accisam crebrisque bipennibus instant
eruere agricolae certatim; illa usque minatur
et tremefacta comam concusso vertice nutat,
630 vulneribus donec paulatim evicta supremum
congemuit traxitque iugis avulsa ruinam.

*Aeneas goes in search of his father, Anchises,
who feels that he is now too old to leave the city.*

Descendo ac ducente deo flammam inter et hostes
expedior: dant tela locum flammaeque recedunt.
atque ubi iam patriae perventum ad limina sedis
635 antiquasque domos, genitor, quem tollere in altos
optabam primum montes primumque petebam,
abnegat excisa vitam producere Troia
exsiliumque pati. 'vos o, quibus integer aevi
sanguis,' ait, 'solidaeque suo stant robore vires,
640 vos agitate fugam.
me si caelicolae voluissent ducere vitam,
has mihi servassent sedes. satis una superque
vidimus excidia et captae superavimus urbi.
sic o sic positum adfati discedite corpus.
645 ipse manu mortem inveniam; miserebitur hostis
exuviasque petet. facilis iactura sepulcri.

24

iam pridem invisus divis et inutilis annos
demoror, ex quo me divum pater atque hominum rex
fulminis adflavit ventis et contigit igni.'

In frustration Aeneas is ready to go and rejoin the fight.

650   Talia perstabat memorans fixusque manebat.
nos contra effusi lacrimis coniunxque Creusa
Ascaniusque omnisque domus, ne vertere secum
cuncta pater fatoque urgenti incumbere vellet.
abnegat inceptoque et sedibus haeret in isdem.
655   rursus in arma feror mortemque miserrimus opto.
nam quod consilium aut quae iam fortuna dabatur?
'mene efferre pedem, genitor, te posse relicto
sperasti tantumque nefas patrio excidit ore?
si nihil ex tanta superis placet urbe relinqui,
660   et sedet hoc animo perituraeque addere Troiae
teque tuosque iuvat: patet isti ianua leto,
iamque aderit multo Priami de sanguine Pyrrhus,
natum ante ora patris, patrem qui obtruncat ad aras.
hoc erat, alma parens, quod me per tela, per ignes
665   eripis, ut mediis hostem in penetralibus utque
Ascanium patremque meum iuxtaque Creusam
alterum in alterius mactatos sanguine cernam?
arma, viri, ferte arma; vocat lux ultima victos.
reddite me Danais; sinite instaurata revisam
670   proelia. numquam omnes hodie moriemur inulti.'

Creusa, Aeneas' wife, pleads with him not to leave them;
her pleas are reinforced by two omens which even win Anchises over.

Hinc ferro accingor rursus clipeoque sinistram
.insertabam aptans meque extra tecta ferebam.
ecce autem complexa pedes in limine coniunx
haerebat, parvumque patri tendebat Iulum:
675   'si periturus abis, et nos rape in omnia tecum;
sin aliquam expertus sumptis spem ponis in armis,
hanc primum tutare domum. cui parvus Iulus,
cui pater et coniunx quondam tua dicta relinquor?'
talia vociferans gemitu tectum omne replebat,
680   cum subitum dictuque oritur mirabile monstrum.
namque manus inter maestorumque ora parentum

25

ecce levis summo de vertice visus Iuli
fundere lumen apex, tactuque innoxia molles
lambere flamma comas et circum tempora pasci.
685 nos pavidi trepidare metu crinemque flagrantem
excutere et sanctos restinguere fontibus ignes.
at pater Anchises oculos ad sidera laetus
extulit et caelo palmas cum voce tetendit:
'Iuppiter omnipotens, precibus si flecteris ullis,
690 aspice nos, hoc tantum, et si pietate meremur,
da deinde augurium, pater, atque haec omina firma.'
vix ea fatus erat senior, subitoque fragore
intonuit laevum, et de caelo lapsa per umbras
stella facem ducens multa cum luce cucurrit.
695 illam summa super labentem culmina tecti
cernimus Idaea claram se condere silva
signantemque vias; tum longo limite sulcus
dat lucem et late circum loca sulphure fumant.
hic vero victus genitor se tollit ad auras
700 adfaturque deos et sanctum sidus adorat.
'iam iam nulla mora est; sequor et qua ducitis adsum,
di patrii; servate domum, servate nepotem.
vestrum hoc augurium, vestroque in numine Troia est.
cedo equidem nec, nate, tibi comes ire recuso.'

*Aeneas sets out for the mountains, carrying his father
and holding his son by the hand; Creusa follows behind.*

705   Dixerat ille, et iam per moenia clarior ignis
auditur, propiusque aestus incendia volvunt.
'ergo age, care pater, cervici imponere nostrae;
ipse subibo umeris nec me labor iste gravabit;
quo res cumque cadent, unum et commune periclum,
710 una salus ambobus erit. mihi parvus Iulus
sit comes, et longe servet vestigia coniunx.
vos, famuli, quae dicam animis advertite vestris.
est urbe egressis tumulus templumque vetustum
desertae Cereris, iuxtaque antiqua cupressus
715 religione patrum multos servata per annos.
hanc ex diverso sedem veniemus in unam.
tu, genitor, cape sacra manu patriosque penates,
me bello e tanto digressum et caede recenti

26

attrectare nefas, donec me flumine vivo
720 abluero.'
haec fatus latos umeros subiectaque colla
veste super fulvique insternor pelle leonis,
succedoque oneri; dextrae se parvus Iulus
implicuit sequiturque patrem non passibus aequis;
725 pone subit coniunx. ferimur per opaca locorum,
et me, quem dudum non ulla iniecta movebant
tela neque adverso glomerati ex agmine Grai,
nunc omnes terrent aurae, sonus excitat omnis
suspensum et pariter comitique onerique timentem.

Aeneas arrives at the appointed place outside the city
only to find that Creusa is missing.

730 Iamque propinquabam portis omnemque videbar
evasisse viam, subito cum creber ad aures
visus adesse pedum sonitus, genitorque per umbram
prospiciens 'nate' exclamat 'fuge, nate; propinquant.
ardentes clipeos atque aera micantia cerno.'
735 hic mihi nescio quod trepido male numen amicum
confusam eripuit mentem. namque avia cursu
dum sequor et nota excedo regione viarum,
heu misero coniunx fatone erepta Creusa
substitit, erravitne via seu lassa resedit,
740 incertum; nec post oculis est reddita nostris.
nec prius amissam respexi animumve reflexi
quam tumulum antiquae Cereris sedemque sacratam
venimus: hic demum collectis omnibus una
defuit, et comites natumque virumque fefellit.
745 quem non incusavi amens hominumque deorumque,
aut quid in eversa vidi crudelius urbe?
Ascanium Anchisenque patrem Teucrosque penates
commendo sociis et curva valle recondo;
ipse urbem repeto et cingor fulgentibus armis.
750 stat casus renovare omnes omnemque reverti
per Troiam et rursus caput obiectare periclis.

While retracing his steps through the city, Aeneas is met by Creusa's ghost
which reveals that Aeneas is to go to a new land in the west without her.

Principio muros obscuraque limina portae,

qua gressum extuleram, repeto et vestigia retro
observata sequor per noctem et lumine lustro:
755   horror ubique animo, simul ipsa silentia terrent.
inde domum, si forte pedem, si forte tulisset,
me refero: inruerant Danai et tectum omne tenebant.
ilicet ignis edax summa ad fastigia vento
volvitur; exsuperant flammae, furit aestus ad auras.
760   procedo et Priami sedes arcemque reviso:
et iam porticibus vacuis Iunonis asylo
custodes lecti Phoenix et dirus Vlixes
praedam adservabant. huc undique Troia gaza
incensis erepta adytis, mensaeque deorum
765   crateresque auro solidi, captivaque vestis
congeritur. pueri et pavidae longo ordine matres
stant circum.
ausus quin etiam voces iactare per umbram
implevi clamore vias, maestusque Creusam
770   nequiquam ingeminans iterumque iterumque vocavi.
quaerenti et tectis urbis sine fine ruenti
infelix simulacrum atque ipsius umbra Creusae
visa mihi ante oculos et nota maior imago.
obstipui, steteruntque comae et vox faucibus haesit.
775   tum sic adfari et curas his demere dictis:
'quid tantum insano iuvat indulgere dolori,
o dulcis coniunx? non haec sine numine divum
eveniunt; nec te hinc comitem asportare Creusam
fas, aut ille sinit superi regnator Olympi.
780   longa tibi exsilia et vastum maris aequor arandum,
et terram Hesperiam venies, ubi Lydius arva
inter opima virum leni fluit agmine Thybris:
illic res laetae regnumque et regia coniunx
parta tibi; lacrimas dilectae pelle Creusae.
785   non ego Myrmidonum sedes Dolopumve superbas
aspiciam aut Grais servitum matribus ibo,
Dardanis et divae Veneris nurus;
sed me magna deum genetrix his detinet oris.
iamque vale et nati serva communis amorem.'
790   haec ubi dicta dedit, lacrimantem et multa volentem
dicere deseruit, tenuesque recessit in auras.
ter conatus ibi collo dare bracchia circum;
ter frustra comprensa manus effugit imago,

par levibus ventis volucrique simillima somno.
795 sic demum socios consumpta nocte reviso.

Aeneas returns to find that a large number of refugees have gathered;
he lifts up his father again and sets out with his followers for the mountains.

Atque hic ingentem comitum adfluxisse novorum
invenio admirans numerum, matresque virosque,
collectam exsilio pubem, miserabile vulgus.
undique convenere animis opibusque parati
800 in quascumque velim pelago deducere terras.
iamque iugis summae surgebat Lucifer Idae
ducebatque diem, Danaique obsessa tenebant
limina portarum, nec spes opis ulla dabatur.
cessi et sublato montes genitore petivi.

'SUBLATO MONTIS GENITORE PETIVI'
Aeneas sets out, carrying Anchises and holding Iulus by the hand.
(Painted terracotta from Pompeii.)

29

ABBREVIATIONS

abl.	ablative	n.	neuter
abs.	absolute	neg.	negative
acc.	accusative	nom.	nominative
adj.	adjective	num.	numerical
adjs.	adjectives	obj.	object
adv.	adverb	object.	objective
alternat.	alternative	objs.	objects
c.	common	part.	particle
cf.	compare	partic.	participle
conj.	conjunction	partics.	participles
dat.	dative	pass.	passive
defect.	defective	perf.	perfect
demons.	demonstrative	perfs.	perfects
distrib.	distributive	pl.	plural
f.	feminine	pluperf.	pluperfect
fut.	future	predic.	predicative
futs.	futures	prep.	preposition
gen.	genitive	pres.	present
Gk.	Greek	pron.	pronoun
		quest.	question
imperat.	imperative	sg.	singular
imperats.	imperatives	subj.	subjunctive
imperf.	imperfect	subject.	subjective
impers.	impersonal	subjs.	subjunctives
ind.	indirect	superl.	superlative
indecl.	indeclinable	syll.	syllable
indef.	indefinite	voc.	vocative
indic.	indicative		
infin.	infinitive		
infins.	infinitives		
interrog.	interrogative		
intrans.	intransitive		
l.	line		
lit.	literally		
locat.	locative		
m.	masculine		

NOTES

1. The first line of this book stresses the sudden hushed silence that fell on the assembled company in queen Dido's palace. Dido had asked Aeneas to tell her about the capture of Troy and his wanderings. **conticuere**: shortened form of *conticuerunt*; note the perfect tense to convey the sudden silence. **intenti...tenebant**: note the change of tense to emphasise the audience's concentration, 'and kept their heads still in concentration'.

2. **pater**: Aeneas is not only the father of Ascanius; here he has the responsibility of being father of his people. **toro**: a banquet had been in progress. **orsus**: from *ordior*, supply *est*, as often in poetry. **alto**: with *toro* 'the top couch'; a mark of honour shown to Aeneas.

3. **infandum**:'unspeakable'; note the stress on this very strong word which literally means 'not to be told'. **iubes**: supply *me* as an object. This sentence has a succession of words denoting sorrow.

4ff. **ut**: 'how'. **eruerint**: perf. subj. for the ind. quest.; the tense stresses the completeness of the action. **quaeque...miserrima**: 'and the most pitiable things which'. **quorum**: refers again to *miserrima*. **pars...fui**: not a boast but a fact and a guarantee of the truth of his story, 'I was greatly involved'.

6f. **quis**: with *Myrmidonum Dolopumve*. **talia fando**: lit. 'with saying such things', i.e. 'while telling such things'; *fando* is the gerund of *for* 'I tell'. **miles**: supply *quis,* 'which soldier'. Ulysses had a reputation in Roman literature for deceit and brutality. **Ulixi**: gen. sg.

8. **temperet**: imperf. subj. 'could refrain'. Aeneas suggests that even the most savage of the Greeks would have been affected by the horrors of Troy's capture. **nox...somnos**: Aeneas is reluctant to start and suggests that the night is too far gone. Like the dawn, darkness was thought to come up over the sky and then go down leaving light behind. **caelo**: as often in poetry a preposition is omitted, 'from the sky'.

9. The alliteration of 's' and the progressively shorter words at the end of the line reflect the idea of drowsiness. **somnos**: pl. for sg.

10. **tantus amor**: supply *est tibi,* 'you have such a great love'; in poetry followed by the infin. **casus**: acc. pl. with *nostros*.

11. **breviter**: not to be taken literally; the story fills the whole of this book and the next. **laborem**: often in poetry 'pain, agony'.

12. **horret**: originally used to describe the way hair stands on end. **luctu**: *a*

31

omitted. **refugit**: perf. tense, 'has recoiled'.

13. Note the emphasis on the demoralised state of the Greeks; both phrases begin with the letter *f*. **fracti...repulsi**: describes *ductores*; this double description gives the human reason (*fracti bello*) and the divine one (*repulsi fatis*).

14. **Danaum**: gen. pl. for *Danaorum*. **tot**: with *annis*; it was now the tenth year since the siege of Troy began.

15. **instar**: an indecl. neuter noun describing *equum*, 'the size of'. Note the impact of the description; first it is massive, then there is help from a goddess. Only after that do we get the material and alleged motive. The effect is to suggest that it was something supernatural. Pallas not only favoured the Greeks, she was goddess of wisdom and handicrafts. According to Homer (*Odyssey* VIII. 493) the horse was Ulysses' idea, built by Epeos with the help of Athene.

16. **costas**: 'ribs'; this word is used of the ribs of ships or baskets. **intexunt**: a metaphor from weaving, 'they interlace'; the ribs are the vertical strands and the planks (*secta abiete*) horizontal. **secta abiete**: lit. 'with cut pine', i.e. 'with planks of pine wood'. The *i* of *abiete* is here a consonant making the word scan as a dactyl.

17. **pro reditu**: 'for their safe return'. **simulant**: supply *eum esse*, 'they pretend that it is'. **ea fama**: 'that [is] the rumour [that]'.

18. **huc**: i.e. 'into this' with *includunt*. **sortiti**: partic. of *sortior*, lit. 'having chosen at random' but here 'having selected'. **delecta virum corpora**: obj. of *includunt*; lit. 'chosen bodies of men', i.e. 'chosen men'; **virum**: gen. pl. for *virorum*. **furtim**: with *includunt*.

19. **caeco lateri**: dat., common in Virgil for *in* with acc.

20. **uterumque**: the horse is described as a pregnant animal that will give birth to its dangerous offspring. **armato milite**: a collective sg., lit. 'with armed soldiery', i.e. 'with armed soldiers'. They are unnamed shadowy figures until they emerge in Troy, see line 261.

21. **in conspectu**: i.e. in sight of Troy. **Tenedos**: this island is a few miles off the coast. **fama**: abl.

22. **dives opum**: 'rich in resources'. **Priami**: gen. with *regna*. **regna**: nom. pl.; poets often used plurals for singulars, here 'the kingdom'.

23. **nunc**: 'but now'. **tantum**: here adv. 'only'. **male fida**: *male* makes *fida* negative, 'treacherous'. **carinis**: lit. 'for keels', i.e. 'for ships'; poets often used a part of something to stand for the whole. This is called synecdoche.

24. **provecti**: the passive of *veho* is commonly used for travelling on some means of transport, 'having sailed' with *huc*. **se**: with *condunt*, 'hide themselves'.

25. **rati**: supply *sumus*, and *eos* with the infins. **vento**: abl., lit.'with the wind',

i.e. 'on a favourable wind'. Note the abrupt start to this line; the first
reaction of the Trojans was that they had gone. **Mycenas**: = 'Greece'; the
particular for the general. This speculation seems to be confirmed by
Sinon, see l. 180.

26. **omnis Teucria**: i.e. not just the city, but the whole countryside. **longo
luctu**: *a* or *e* omitted. **se solvit**: 'relaxed'. Note how the spondees in this
line mark the memories of grief but the next two lines reflect the
increasing joy with increasing dactyls. The Trojans, in contrast to the
Greeks who deviously hide men away, naively open up their city.

27. **panduntur portae**: a grand phrase (note the repeated '*p*') to indicate an
official opening. **iuvat**: supply *nos*, 'we are delighted'; compare modern
guided tours of world war battle sites.

28. **desertosque...relictum**: note the chiasmus.

29f. **hic...hic**: Virgil imagines Trojans walking about pointing out the various
parts of the Greek camp. **tendebat**: this verb goes with the two sg.
subjects, *manus* and *Achilles*; supply *tentoria* 'tents'. **locus**: supply *est*.
acie: *in* omitted; *acies* denotes a formal pitched battle. **solebant**: subject
is 'the Greeks'.

31. **pars**: i.e. 'some'; note that Virgil uses a singular and then a plural verb.
Minervae: a so-called objective gen., 'gift to Minerva'. **innuptae**: Minerva or Pallas (see l. 15) was a maiden goddess. To the Greeks she was
known as Athena Parthenos and a temple to her, the Parthenon, still stands
on the acropolis at Athens. **exitiale**: a word laden with doom; Aeneas
speaks with the wisdom of hindsight.

32. **molem**: again the vast size of the horse is emphasised (see l. 15).
primusque Thymoetes: 'and Thymoetes is the first to'. There is a legend
that Thymoetes' wife and son were put to death by Priam; so Thymoetes
had a possible motive for treachery.

33. **duci**: pres. infin. pass. of *duco* 'to be led'; supply *eum* to form an ind.
statement (acc. + infin.) after *hortatur*. In prose *hortor* would normally
take *ut* + subj. **arce**: *in* omitted.

34. **iam**: 'by now'. **ferebant**: describes the direction the fates were taking
things, 'were tending'. Note a human and a divine reason again (see l. 13).

35. **quorum...menti**: supply *ei* and *est*, lit. 'those (*ei*) to whose mind (*quorum
menti*) there is a better opinion'.

36f. **pelago**: dat. for *in pelagus*, see *caeco lateri* (l. 19). **Danaum**: gen. pl. for
Danaorum. **insidias...dona**: obj. pl. nouns for sg.; they both refer to the
horse. **iubent**: supply some obj. such as *nos*, 'they (i.e. Capys and the
sensible people) order us to hurl...or burn...'.

38. **terebrare...temptare**: Virgil is describing holes being bored into its side

and then something like spears being pushed into the holes. Perhaps *temptare* means 'to probe for'.

39. **incertum**: with *vulgus*. **studia**: 'factions' or 'sides'.

40. **magna...caterva**: abl. abs. 'with a great crowd accompanying him'. This sentence emphasises Laocoon's eagerness to speak with *ardens* and *decurrit*, and the fact that he shouts to the rest long before he reaches them. Unlike the *incertum vulgus* he knows his mind. On the citadel is probably where the temples of Pallas and Apollo were.

42. **procul**: supply a verb such as *clamat*. Verbs of speaking are frequently omitted before direct speech in poetry and even in prose.
quae: supply *est*, 'what is [this]...'. Laocoon's speech is beautifully composed: an attention-grabbing vocative, a series of rhetorical questions, a clear assessment of the situation and a memorable proverb.

43. **avectos**: supply *esse* to make an infin. The parts of *sum* are very often omitted even when they form part of passive verbs as here.

44. **dolis**: abl. required by *carere*; pl. noun perhaps for 'acts of deceit'. **Danaum**: gen. pl. for *Danaorum*; in contrast to *Minervae* (l. 31) this is the more normal subjective gen. **sic...Ulixes**: supply *est vobis*. For Romans Ulysses was the greatest exponent of Greek cunning. Laocoon does not know that the horse was the product of Ulysses' cunning but his instinct is good. Perhaps Ulysses inside hears him.

45f. **hoc...haec**: note the repetition, no doubt to indicate a gesture. **machina**: 'contraption' (Austin) or 'engine of war'; this is the general word in Latin for the various devices used by Roman armies to besiege cities. **in**: 'against', 'to threaten'.

47. **inspectura, ventura**: fut. partics. to express purpose, 'to spy on, to come'; the horse is viewed as a *turris* built to dominate the beseiged city and allow the attackers to fire arrows into it. **urbi**: dat. for *in* + acc. 'onto the city'; see *caeco lateri* (l. 19) and *pelago* (l. 36).

48. **aliquis**: 'some other'. **latet**: often used of trickery or deception, 'lurks'. **error**: 'deception'. **equo**: note the emphatic start of this sentence 'the horse, don't trust it'. **ne credite**: *ne* + the imperat. is used in poetry for *noli* + infin.

49. **et**: 'even'. **timeo...ferentes**: this has become proverbial in English.

50. **sic fatus**: *fatus* from *for* 'I speak'. Since the poem was written to be read aloud, Virgil is telling his audience that Laocoon's speech has finished.

51. **feri**: gen. sg. 'of the beast'. **curvam...alvum**: 'the belly curved with jointed timbers'.

52. **stetit**: 'it stuck'. **illa**: 'it', i.e. the spear. **tremens**: 'vibrating'. **utero recusso**: abl. abs. 'when the womb was made to reverberate'. The words *curvam* *alvum, utero, gemitum dedere* are words of childbirth; but the 'pregnancy' of this horse will result in death, not life, for the Trojans.

53. **insonuere, dedere**: shortened forms of *insonuerunt* and *dederunt*. **cavae cavernae**: repetition of a syllable to suggest an echo.

54. **deum**: gen. pl. for *deorum*. **mens**: 'their intention'. **laeva**: 'unfavourable', 'unpropitious'.

55. **impulerat**: subject is Laocoon; supply *nos*. Normally this would have been a pluperf. subj. to balance *fuisset* (l. 54); this pluperf. tense makes Laocoon's attempt seem to have only just failed, 'he had driven us'. **ferro**: 'with our swords'.

56. **staret**: imperf. subj. 'would be standing'. **arx alta**: here voc. as *maneres* shows, 'you, high citadel'. Addressing the citadel adds to the pathos of Aeneas' reflection; to switch from a narrative and address an inanimate object in this way is known as apostrophe.

57. **ecce**: Virgil uses this word to mark a change of scene, a shift in attention or a sudden interruption, see also lines 318 and 526. The arrival of Sinon is a crucial distraction that prevents Laocoon convincing the Trojans. Note that we meet the prisoner before those bringing him, which suggests that he was in the centre of the group. The basic elements of this huge sentence are: *Dardanidae pastores trahebant iuvenem ad regem*. **manus**: acc. pl. with *revinctum* describing the part affected. **iuvenem revinctum**: lit. 'a young man tied as regards his hands', more naturally 'a young man with his hands tied'.

58. **regem**: i.e. King Priam. **trahebant**: Sinon was pretending to struggle.

59. **qui**: refers to *iuvenem* and is the subject of *obtulerat* (l. 61). **se ignotum ultro obtulerat**: 'had voluntarily (*ultro*) offered himself, a stranger'. **venientibus**: supply *eis*, 'to them as they were coming along'.

60. **ut**: take this word first in the line; it has been postponed in order to emphasise *hoc ipsum*. **hoc ipsum**: 'just this', i.e. his arrest and arrival in Troy.

61. **fidens animi**: *animi* is a gen., 'confident in spirit'. **in utrumque**: supply *casum*, 'for either outcome'; explained by the next line.

63. **visendi studio**: lit. 'with eagerness of looking at', more naturally 'in eagerness to look at him'. The eagerness and excitement of the Trojans are suggested by a number of words: *undique, certant, circumfusa, ruit, studio* and *visendi*.

64. **circumfusa**: 'crowding around'. **certant**: note the switch to a pl. verb. **capto**: partic. used as a noun, 'the prisoner'.

65. **accipe**: 'hear' or 'listen to'. The two imperats. *accipe* and *disce* are addressed to Dido. **Danaum**: gen. pl. for *Danaorum*. **crimine...uno**:

'from one charge', i.e. from the accusation against one man, Sinon the captive.

66. **omnes**: supply *insidias*, 'the whole stratagem'; see Williams. There are 55 part lines in the whole Aeneid with more (10) occurring in this book than in any other. It is probable that Virgil would have completed them before publishing his poem, if he had had the opportunity.

67. **namque**: a stronger form of *nam*. **ut**: 'when' or 'as'. **turbatus**: Sinon has been roughly handled by the *pastores*.

68. **circumspexit**: this line has a very unusual ending since Virgil uses a spondee in the fifth foot. It slows the line down and helps us to visualise the slow deliberate way Sinon looked round at the crowd.

69. **heu**: the combination of this word and the use of questions makes Sinon's speech seem all the more tragic, which is what he wanted. **quae**: with *tellus*, 'what land'; supply *potest accipere* from the second question. **quae**: n. pl. with *aequora*, 'what seas'.

71. **cui**: 'for whom'; Sinon is referring to himself. **locus**: supply *est*. **super**: adv. here, 'in addition'.

72. **sanguine**: he is referring to his own blood.

73. **quo**: a connecting relative with *gemitu*, 'by this lamentation'. **conversi**: supply *sunt*. **animi**: supply *nostri*, 'our feelings'. **compressus et**: *et* has been postponed and should be translated first; supply *est* to *compressus*. **omnis impetus**: 'all aggression'. Notice here the naive friendliness of the Trojans in strong contrast to the calculated deceit of Sinon and the Greeks.

74. **hortamur**: supply *eum* as its obj. **fari**: the infin. of *for* 'I say'; in poetry *hortor* is often followed by the infin. instead of the subj. as in prose. **quo sanguine cretus**: supply *sit* for an ind. quest., 'from what blood he was born'.

75. **ferat**: subj. for another ind. quest., 'what information he is bringing'. **memoret**: subj. 'let him relate'. **quae**: supply *sibi*, lit. 'what reliance there is to him as a captive', or more naturally 'on what he as a captive relies'.

76. This line which also appears as line 612 in Book 3 is not in some of the best manuscripts and so perhaps ought to be ignored here. **deposita...formidine**: an abl. abs., 'at last having laid aside his fear'. **haec**: n. pl. object of *fatur*.

77. Sinon's opening words cleverly emphasise *cuncta* and *vera*. **cuncta**: with *vera* 'the whole truth'. **equidem**: with *fatebor*, 'I will indeed confess'. **fuerit quodcumque**: 'whatever will be [the result]'; *fuerit* is a perf. subj. Sinon in his speech plays on the emotions of his audience with such words and phrases as *fuerit quodcumque* (l. 77), *miserum* (l. 79), *pauper pater* (l. 87) and *adflictus...trahebam* (l. 92). Despite his elaborate profession of honesty and his lengthy speech Sinon reveals very little about himself;

he did not say, perhaps wisely, that he was a full cousin of Ulysses.

78.   **me**: supply *esse*.

79f.   **nec**: with *finget* (l. 80). **miserum**: this adj. is predicative, i.e. it goes after *finxit Sinonem*, 'has made Sinon wretched'. **finxit, finget**: *fingo* lit. 'I mould, fashion' here 'I make'. **vanum, mendacem**: these adjs. too are predicative and in strong contrast to *miserum*; insert 'but' before *vanum*. **finget**: supply *eum*. **improba**: describing *fortuna*, 'she, however malicious, will not also make him'.

81.   **fando**: gerund of *for*, lit. 'by talking', i.e. 'in conversation' or 'in discussion'. **aliquod**: with *nomen*, 'some mention of the name'. **si forte**: this is where the grammar of the sentence begins. This complex and convoluted sentence reflects Sinon's deliberately devious style. He does not want to give plain answers to anything so creates a smokescreen of irrelevant background detail.

82.   **Belidae**: gen. sg. of *Belides* with *Palamedis*, 'of Palamedes descendant of Belus'; such names are called patronymics. **incluta...gloria**: *fama* is abl. sg., the other two nouns are nom. sg., 'renown famous by report'.

83ff.   **quem**: refers to Palamedes. Take the words in this order to begin with: *quem Pelasgi demisere insontem neci*. **demisere**: shortened form of *demiserunt*. **neci**: dat. sg. for *ad necem*. **falsa...proditione**: 'under a false [charge of] treachery'. **indicio**: the *indicium* was a letter supposedly written by Priam but forged by Ulysses and hidden in Palamedes' tent. Note the repetition of *in-* and the two elisions which stress the terrible injustice. **quia**: this is the real reason according to Sinon that Palamedes was killed, which Virgil places next to the false evidence. **cassum lumine**: supply 'but' before this strong contrast and *eum*, 'him deprived of the light' i.e. dead. In Latin poetry the light of day often stands for life and the darkness of night for death.

86.   **illi me**: note how Virgil places the two men side by side like true comrades in arms, with *illi* emphasised; 'it was to him that my father sent me'.

87.   **pauper**: Sinon looking for sympathy says that his poor father sent him away to the war as a teenager (*primis ab annis*) along with an older relative. Note that Sinon does not name his father. **in arma**: with *huc misit*, 'sent me here to war'.

88.   **stabat**: the subject of this is Palamedes. **regno**: for *in regno*, with *incolumis*, 'safe in his royal power'.

89.   **conciliis**: for *in conciliis*. **et nos**: 'I too'; Latin poets often used pl. pronouns for sg.

90.   **invidia**: abl. sg., with *pellacis Ulixi*.

91.   **haud ignota**: n. pl. and a double negative to give a strong positive 'well known things'. **concessit**: the subject is Palamedes. **superis ab oris**: 'from the shores above', i.e. from life.

92. **trahebam vitam**: 'I dragged out a life'.

93. **insontis**: with *amici*. **indignabar mecum**: 'I brooded with indignation inside myself at'.

94. **demens**: with 'I' of *tacui*. **nec tacui**: note the sudden change of tense indicating an outburst on one occasion. **me**: this is object after *promisi* (l. 96). **qua**: a rare nom. f. sg. of *quis*, with *fors*, 'some fortune'. **tulisset**: this pluperf. subj. represents a fut. perf. tense in what Sinon actually said, 'if some fortune brought it about'.

95. **remeassem**: a shortened pluperf. subj. for *remeavissem*; this subj. is the same as *tulisset*, 'if I returned'. **victor**: 'as victor'. **patrios Argos**: 'my native Argos'.

96. **promisi ultorem**: with *me* (l. 94), 'I promised myself as an avenger'. **odia aspera**: note the plural, 'harsh feelings of hatred'. **movi**: 'I stirred up'.

97. **hinc**: 'from this', i.e. from this action or time; note the repeats of *hinc* for emphasis. **prima mali labes**: *labes* is the noun connected to the verb *labor*, 'the first slip to disaster'; supply *erat*.

98f. **terrere, spargere, quaerere**: historic infins.; translate as imperfect tenses. **terrere**: supply *me*. **novis**: here 'fresh'. **spargere**: probably a metaphor of sowing. **voces**: 'remarks'. **et quaerere conscius arma**: 'and as a conspirator (*conscius*) looked for means [against me]'; *arma* normally refers to weapons, but here, as the next line shows, it refers to the help of a prophet.

100. **enim**: here 'indeed', corroborating the previous statement. **Calchante ministro**: abl. abs., 'with Calchas as his assistant'; Calchas was the prophet to the Greek army. Note how the story is cleverly halted when the interest of the audience has been roused.

101. **quid**: 'why'; also in line 102. **haec**: with *ingrata*. **revolvo**: 'I go over again'.

102. **habetis uno ordine**: *in* is omitted, 'you hold in one category', i.e. 'you consider alike'.

103. **id**: 'that', i.e. Greek. **audire**: this word can be used as the passive of *appellare*, 'to be called'. **iamdudum**: this word lit. means 'long since' or 'long ago' and here refers to a punishment due long ago; translate with *poenas* as 'long overdue'.

104. **velit, mercentur**: pres. subjs. 'would wish' and 'would buy'. This is the second part of a fut. hypothetical sentence with the first part suppressed. The missing part is something like 'If the Greeks were to find out I had been captured'. **Ithacus**: a mark of Sinon's pretended hatred of Ulysses – he does not use his name. **magno**: abl., supply *pretio*, 'at a great price'.

105. Aeneas speaking again. **Tum vero**: a solemn expression often to signpost a crisis (e.g. lines 228, 309, 624). **ardemus**: a very strong substitute for *volumus*, 'we ardently desire'.

106. **ignari**: a nom. pl. adj. describing the subject of *ardemus*.

107. **prosequitur**: subject is Sinon. **pavitans**: part of Sinon's act. **ficto pectore**: 'from his false heart'.

108. **fugam**: obj. of *moliri*. **cupiere**: shortened form of *cupiverunt*. **Troia relicta**: abl. abs., but translate as 'to leave Troy and...'.

109. **moliri et discedere**: two infins. after *cupiere*. **fessi longo bello**: describing *Danai* and giving the reason for their action.

110. **fecissent**: pluperf. subj. for a wish that something had been done but was not. **aspera ponti hiems**: 'the rough stormy weather at sea'; **ponti**: is possibly locat. rather than gen.

111. **euntes**: 'just as they were going'.

112. Sinon refers to the horse for the first time. **hic**: with *equus*. **trabibus...acernis**: for *contextus*, see note on *intexunt* (l. 16); here Virgil describes the horse as built with maple planks whereas in line 16 he talks of pine and later in line 186 it will be oak. This is not a matter of inconsistency but rather that Virgil prefers a particular wood instead of just wood and then likes to give variety to his poetry. This is seen also in the variety of words he uses for the Greeks.

113. **toto aethere**: *in* is usually omitted in phrases with *totus*, even in prose, 'over the whole sky'.

114. **suspensi**: adj. describing the subject of *mittimus*, 'in doubt'. **scitantem**: from *scitor*, 'seeking to know'.

115. **adytis**: *ex* is omitted.

116. **sanguine...et virgine**: a hendiadys, 'with the blood of a girl'. **placastis**: shortened form of *placavistis*. **virgine caesa**: the girl sacrificed to obtain a wind for the Greek fleet was Iphigeneia, who was killed at Aulis by her own father Agamemnon, king of Mycenae and leader of the Greek army, when the Greeks sailed for Troy 10 years earlier.

117. **cum**: 'when'.

118. **sanguine**: note the position, balancing line 116. **quaerendi reditus**: supply *sunt*; *reditus* is a pl. noun for sg., 'a return must be sought'. **litandum**: supply *est*; *lito* is used for making sacrifices or offerings which ensure a favourable result, 'divine favour must be gained'.

119. **Argolica**: note the position of this word to emphasise the horror; the Greeks have to sacrifice one of their own number. **quae vox ut**: 'when this report'; note the repetition of the letter *v*. **vulgi**: gen. sg. with *ad aures*, 'of the crowd'.

120. **obstipuere**: shortened form of *obstipuerunt*. **per ima ossa**: 'through their innermost bones'.
121. **cui fata parent**: lit. 'for whom are the fates making preparations'; this and the following clause are indirect questions and therefore the subj. is used. According to Sinon the Greeks are anxiously asking themselves these things.
122. **hic**: of time, 'at this point'. **Ithacus**: see note to line 104. **magno tumultu**: *in* is omitted, 'amid the great uproar'. **Calchanta**: the so-called Greek acc. sg. of *Calchas*.The prophet is needed to interpret the god's purpose (*numina* line 123). Note how Sinon paints Ulysses as a noisy, vulgar, violent thug.
123. **quae...divum**: an ind. quest. after *flagitat*; *divum* gen. pl. for *divorum*, 'what are those divine purposes of the gods'.
124. **et multi canebant**: 'and many began to prophesy'; the prophecies of the gods were customarily chanted in verse so *cano* can mean 'I prophesy'. **mihi**: 'for me', i.e. 'against me'.
125. **crudele artificis scelus**: 'a cruel crime of the schemer'. **taciti**: lit.'silently', i.e. not saying anything because of fear. **ventura**: lit. 'the things about to come', or in better English 'what was about to happen'.
126. **bis quinos**: poetical expression for *decem*. **ille**: i.e. Calchas. **tectus**: lit. 'covered', better 'shut up'; Calchas was shut up in his tent and concealing his thoughts.
127. **quemquam**: 'anyone'; *quisquam* is used in negative sentences and this sentence is made negative by *recusat*.
128. **vix tandem**: 'finally reluctantly'; this phrase emphasises the reluctance of Calchas. **Ithaci**: see the note to line 104.
129. **composito**: 'by agreement'; so Calchas was in the plot all the time. **rumpit vocem**: lit. 'breaks out an utterance', i.e. 'breaks his silence'. **arae**: dat. sg.
130f. A bitter comment on human nature. **adsensere**: for *adsenserunt*. **quae**: supply *ea*, 'those things which'; *quae* is obj. of *timebat*. **unius...tulere**: *tulere* for *tulerunt*; 'they tolerated when turned (*conversa*) into the destruction (*in exitium*) of one wretched person'. **conversa**: with *quae* in previous line.
132. **dies**: is f. here. **sacra**: explained in the next line. **parari**: historic infin., translate as *parata sunt*.
133. **salsae fruges**: meal mixed with salt which was sprinkled on the head of the sacrificial victim. **vittae**: bands which were put around the head of the victim. **tempora**: '[my] temples'.
134. **eripui me**: 'I snatched myself'; note the emphatic position of the verb

stressing the speed of the action. Sinon does not go into details about this unlikely escape.

135. **limoso lacu:** *in* omitted. **obscurus:** 'hidden'.

136. **delitui:** Virgil uses this word of a snake in the *Georgics*; snake imagery is central in this book. **dum vela darent:** note the imperf. subj. indicating purpose, 'until they should set sail'. Both this clause and the following one are indirect speech reporting what Sinon thought as he went into hiding: i.e. 'until they set sail (pres. subj.), if only they are going to (fut. perf. tense)'. **si forte dedissent:** the pluperf. subj. is for a fut. perf. tense in the direct form; 'if by any chance they would'.

137. **nec mihi:** supply *est*.

138. Sinon piles on the pathos, though his family are an invention.

139. **quos illi poenas reposcent:** the verb takes a double object, like *doceo*; 'from whom (*quos*) they (*illi*) will demand punishment'; *illi* = the Greeks, quos = his family. **fors et:** 'and maybe'; the *et* emphasises Sinon's pretended fear that revenge may be taken on his family. **nostra:** 'my'.

140. **hanc:** 'this of mine'. **miserorum:** Sinon is describing his family.

141. Note the gross impiety of Sinon appealing to the gods to support his disception. **quod:** adverbial use of *quod*, 'wherefore'. **te:** obj. of *oro*; probably addressing Priam. **per superos et numina:** 'by the gods and divine powers'. **veri:** gen. sg. with *conscia*, 'who know the truth'.

142. **per si qua est quae restet fides:** 'by any faith that remains', on *qua* see note on l. 94. **mortalibus:** dat.

143. **miserere:** sg. imperat. of *misereor*, 'pity'; this verb is followed by the gen. **laborum:** 'troubles'; 'hardships', 'sufferings'; cf. l. 284.

144. **animi...ferentis:** 'a soul enduring things it does not deserve'. Sinon is of course referring to himself and is attempting to gain the pity of his captors.

145. **his lacrimis:** abl., lit. 'by', i.e. 'because of'. **ultro:** this word is used to mark actions which go beyond what is expected; 'what is more, we...'. See also lines 193 and 372.

146. **ipse:** with *Priamus*. **viro:** an example of the so-called ethic dat. equivalent to the gen., 'the man's'. **primus:** with *iubet*, 'is the first to order'. **arta:** with *vincla*.

147. **amicis:** an adj. here.

148. **obliviscere:** sg. imperat. **amissos Graios:** lit. 'the lost Greeks', i.e. 'the Greeks you have lost'. **hinc iam:** of time rather than place, 'from now on'. Priam's openness and kindness in this speech contrast sharply with Sinon's blasphemy, false oaths and feigned sincerity; cf. lines 154ff.

149. **noster:** 'one of us'; these words were the formula used by a general on receiving a deserter. **haec:** obj. of *roganti*, not with *vera*. **edissere vera:**

41

'explain truthfully'.

150f. The five staccato questions indicate excitement. **quo:** 'to what end', or 'for what purpose'. **statuere:** for *statuerunt*. **molem...equi:** note how Priam is stressing the vast size of the horse with the words *molem* and *immanis*; 'this mass of a monstrous horse', i.e. 'this massive and monstrous horse'. **quae religio:** 'what sacred object is it?' The last two questions concern the possible functions of the horse debated by the Trojans earlier.

152. **dixerat:** since the Aeneid was designed to be read aloud, the poet used this word and other phrases to indicate when the direct speech had come to an end. **ille:** i.e. Sinon.

153. **vinclis:** goes closely with *exutas*. **sidera:** 'the sky'; it is daytime.

154. **aeterni ignes:** i.e. the sun, moon and stars.

156. **deum:** for *deorum*. **quas...gessi:** 'which I as a victim wore'. By his elaborate list of holy objects Sinon tries to convince his hearers of his honesty and piety.

157. **fas:** supply *est*. **Graiorum sacrata iura:** 'the hallowed oaths of the Greeks'. Since *fas* refers to divine law and *iura* to human oaths, Sinon claims to have the gods' permission to break the oaths of loyalty which he swore as a Greek soldier.

158. **ferre sub auras:** i.e. 'bring into the open'; an ironic statement since Sinon is setting out to deceive his audience.

159. **si qua tegunt:** *qua* is n. pl. of *quis*, 'whatever they conceal'. **nec:** goes very closely with *teneor*, 'nor am I bound'.

160f. **tu:** with *Troia* (l. 161); a grandiose gesture, to address Troy itself. **modo... maneas:** 'only abide by your promises'; *maneas* and *serves* are pres. subjs. and act as milder imperats. than *mane* and *serva*. **servataque...fidem:** 'and having been kept safe, keep safe your faith [with me]'; Virgil emphasises the bargain Sinon wishes the Trojans to keep by using the same verb twice.

161. **si magna rependam:** 'if I pay you back a great amount'; *rependam* and *feram* before it are both fut. tenses, and refer to the story which Sinon is about to relate.

162. **Danaum:** gen. pl. for *Danaorum*. **coepti....belli:** 'confidence in the war they had undertaken'; *belli* is an objective gen.

163. **auxiliis stetit:** 'was based upon the help'; *auxiliis* is an abl. with *in* omitted. **ex quo:** supply *tempore*, 'since the time when'.

164. **sed enim:** this phrase should be taken first in the sentence; 'but indeed'.

165. **fatale:** with *Palladium*. The Palladium was an image of Pallas which gave protection to the city of Troy; according to Sinon, the Greeks lost the help of Pallas because Ulysses and Diomedes tried to steal it. **avellere adgressi:**

supply *sunt* to *adgressi*, 'attempted to tear out'.
166. **summae:** agrees with *arcis*. **caesis custodibus:** an abl. abs.
167. **corripuere:** for *corripuerunt*.
168. **ausi:** supply *sunt*.
169. **ex illo:** supply *tempore*; this phrase answers *ex quo* (l. 163), 'from that time'. **fluere...referri:** historic infins.; translate as past tenses with *spes Danaum* as the subject, 'ebbed (*fluere*) and slipping away (*retro sublapsa*) was swept off'. This metaphorical description is drawn from the ebbing of a tide; the smoothness of the language here contrasts strongly with the forceful phrases of the next line.
170. **fractae:** supply *sunt*. **aversa:** supply *est*.
171. **ea signa:** 'evidence of that', i.e. signs of her hostile attitude. **nec dubiis monstris:** the negative force of *nec* goes with *dubiis*; 'and with unmistakeable omens'.
172. **positum:** supply *est*. **castris:** *in* omitted. **arsere:** for *arserunt*. This line is an example of parataxis where two clauses are placed one after the other without any indication of their connection; here we would expect *cum* or *ubi* before *arsere*.
173. **luminibus:** abl. 'from its eyes'. **per artus:** 'along its limbs'.
174. **iit:** English would use a more colourful verb, perhaps 'poured'. **ipsa:** 'the goddess herself'. **solo:** abl. 'from the ground'. **mirabile dictu:** *dictu* is the supine of *dico* in its abl. form, lit. 'in telling'; it is used after a few adjs., here 'marvellous to tell'.
175. **emicuit:** Virgil is describing the goddess suddenly appearing and disappearing three times. **parmamque:** 'both a shield'.
176. **extemplo:** with *temptanda*. **temptanda fuga aequora:** *temptanda* is a gerundive agreeing with *aequora, fuga* is abl., supply *esse*; 'that the seas must be risked in flight'. **canit:** 'proclaims'; prophets traditionally gave prophecies in poetic form and quite possibly chanted them.
177. **nec posse exscindi Pergama:** 'and that Troy cannot be razed'.
178. **ni:** = *nisi*. **repetant:** note the pres. subj.; 'they were to seek again'. Sometimes when a war was not going well, Roman generals had to return to Rome to seek fresh omens. Here Virgil attributes a Roman custom to the Greeks and thereby makes the custom seem even more ancient. **reducant:** another pres. subj. **numen:** this refers to the stolen *Palladium*.
179. **quod:** 'which', referring to the *numen*. **pelago:** 'over the sea'. **avexere:** for *avexerunt*.
180. **quod:** an adv. here, 'as to the fact that'. **petiere:** for *petierunt*; subject is 'the Greeks'. **patrias:** Agamemnon, the leader of the army was king of Mycenae, but other sections of the Greek forces came from other places.

Virgil: Aeneid II

181. **comites**: this refers to *deos*; 'as companions', i.e. 'to accompany them'. **pelagoque remenso**: an abl. abs.; *remenso* from *remetior* 'I measure again', i.e. 'when the sea has been recrossed'.

182. **aderunt**: fut. of *adsum*; Sinon for once is telling the truth. **omina**: the omens are the happenings described in lines 172-5.

183. **hanc**: Sinon points to the horse; *hanc* goes with *effigiem*. **moniti**: refers to the subject of *statuere*, i.e. the Greeks. **pro**: 'to atone for'. **laeso**: probably describes *Palladio* and *numine*.

184. **statuere**: for *statuerunt*. **nefas**: 'sacrilege'. **quae...piaret**: the subj. indicates purpose, 'to atone for'.

185. **hanc immensam molem**: refers to *hanc effigiem* and emphasises its huge size.

186. **roboribus textis**: 'with oak-timbers fitted together'. **caelo**: dat. for *ad caelum*. **iussit**: supply *eos*.

187. **ne...posset**: 'so that it could not be'. **recipi...duci**: pass. infins. **portis**: 'by way of the gates', i.e. through the gates.

188. **neu**: this is the short form of *neve*, for *et ne*, 'and so that...it could not', supply *posset* from line 187. **antiqua**: 'traditional'. **sub**: 'under the protection of'. People in the ancient world believed that sacred objects could and did protect their possessors.

189. **nam**: lines 189-194 are reported speech, i.e. 'for he said that if...'; all of Calchas' reported speech is of course bogus. **violasset**: shortened form of *violavisset*. This pluperf. subj. gives the indirect version of what Calchas said; in the direct form a fut. perf. tense would have been used; cf. line 94. **dona Minervae**: an objective gen., 'the gift to Minerva'; referring to the horse.

190f. **magnum exitium futurum**: supply *esse* to make an acc. + infin., 'there would be a great destruction'. **quod omen di convertant**: note the pres. subj. for a wish; 'may the gods turn this omen'. **in ipsum**: refers to Calchas, 'on the man himself'.

192. **ascendisset**: the subject of this is the horse. Note the emphasis marked by *vestris vestram*.

193f. **Asiam venturam**: cf. line 190; supply *esse* to make an acc. + infin., 'Asia would come'. **ultro**: 'unprovoked', marking an action which is beyond what is expected; i.e. not just content with defending itself and driving away the Greeks, Asia would actually invade Greece. **Pelopea**: an adj. going with *moenia*; Pelops was the grandfather of Agamemnon. **ea fata manere**: a second acc. + infin., 'that fate awaited'. This prophecy came true when the Romans, the new Trojans, invaded Greece proper in 199 BC. **nostros nepotes**: Sinon is talking about later generations of Greeks.

44

195. **talibus insidiis, arte**: both nouns abl. 'through such snares and the skill'.
periuri: gen. sg. going with *Sinonis*.
196. **credita**: supply *est*. **res**: 'the story'. **capti**: supply *sumus*; 'we' is the antecedent of *quos*, 'and we were captured...whom'. **coactis**: 'forced', i.e. false.
198. **domuere**: for *domuerunt* from *domo*. **decem**: that was the traditional length of the siege of Troy. Note the steady build up over lines 197-8 from single heroes to the thousand ships and the repetition of *neque...nec* and *non...non*.
199f. Note the alliteration of '*m*' in this line. **hic**: of time rather than place, 'at this point'. **aliud maius**: 'something else greater', i.e. 'something else more significant'. **miseris**: supply *nobis*. **multo magis tremendum**: *multo* is an abl., 'by much', qualifying the comparative adj. i.e. 'much more fearful'; note the emphatic position of *magis*.
201. **ductus sorte**: 'drawn by lot'.
202. **mactabat**: imperf. shows that his sacrifice was interrupted. **ad**: 'at'. The altar must be on the seashore which was the appropriate place to honour Neptune.
203. **ecce...**: signals a sudden shift in the story. The order of the words describing the beginning of this incident is very carefully devised to recreate it as it happened and lend suspense to the description; try to keep the word order in the translation as far as possible. **Tenedo**: foreshadowing the return of the Greek fleet. **tranquilla**: indicates that the danger was totally unexpected. **alta**: a noun here, 'depths'.
205. **incumbunt pelago**: lit. 'lean on the sea', i.e. 'breast the sea'; *pelago* is dat. **pariter**: 'side by side'.
206. **pectora, iubae**: both nouns are subjects of *superant*.
207. Note the frequent 's' sounds. **pars cetera**: 'the rest of them'.
208. **sinuat...terga**: *pars cetera* is still the subject, 'and curves its enormous back in a coil '.
209. **spumante salo**: an abl. abs., 'as the salt sea foams'. Note the alliteration of 's' imitating both the snakes and the frothing sea. **arva**: 'dry land'. **tenebant**: lit. 'they held', i.e. 'they reached'.
210. **ardentesque...suffecti**: *ardentes oculos* is an acc. phrase limiting the meaning of *suffecti*, lit. 'tinged in their blazing eyes', i.e. 'with their blazing eyes tinged'. **igni**: abl. = *igne*.
212. The long description which started with the snakes away in the distance ends with their flickering tongues and hissing mouths. Note the short sentence for the instant reaction of the onlookers. **visu**: an abl. 'by the sight'; this explains *exsangues*. **agmine certo**: a military phrase, perhaps

45

hinting at the Greeks who will shortly return, 'with a unswerving advance'.
213. **Laocoonta**: the so-called Greek acc.
214. **amplexus**: perf. partic. of *amplector*, 'having encircled'.
215. **morsu depascitur**: lit. 'feeds on [them] by biting', i.e. 'devours'.
216. **post**: an adv. marking out the next victim. **ipsum**: i.e. 'Laocoon himself'.
    auxilio: a predic. dat., lit. 'for a help', i.e. 'to help'.
217. Note the interweaving of the metre in this line with dactyl followed by
    spondee twice over and then the sudden arresting pair of monosyllables
    at the end indicating that all three are tightly tied up by the snakes.
218f. **amplexi**: cf. line 214. **medium**: supply *eum*, 'him around the middle'.
    circum: is part of a split compound verb and goes with *dati*; this splitting
    of a compound is called tmesis. Here the verb although passive in form
    has an active meaning and may be an example of a Latin poet copying
    the Greek use of a middle verb, 'having put their scaly backs (*squamea*
    terga) round his neck (*collo*)'. **superant**: emphasises the height of the
    snakes. **capite...altis**: this phrase refers to the snakes and not Laocoon;
    'with their heads and tall necks'.
220. **ille**: note the swift change of subject; 'he', i.e. Laocoon. **simul**: this and
    simul in line 222 mark two actions which are going on at the same time.
221. **vittas**: cf. *ardentes oculos* in line 210; *vittas* limits the extent of *perfusus*,
    lit. 'drenched in his fillets', i.e. 'with his fillets drenched'. Fillets were
    headbands worn by priests as part of their religious dress and so they were
    holy objects and should not be polluted by contact with dirt or filth.
223. **qualis**: technically *est* is needed, but translate as 'like the bellowing'. This
    simile suggests that Laocoon is himself now the sacrificial victim; line
    202 says that he was in the process of sacrificing when this incident
    occurred. **cum**: with perf. tense, 'when'.
224. **incertam**: i.e. the stroke of the axe on its neck had not been delivered firmly
    enough. The escape of a sacrificial victim was a bad omen; also victims
    were supposed to go to their deaths willingly.
225. **lapsu**: with *effugiunt*, 'escape by slithering', i.e. 'they slither away'.
226. **saevaeque...Tritonidis**: i.e. Pallas Athene; she supported the Greeks in the
    war (cf. lines 15 and 163) and evidently sent the snakes to kill Laocoon
    who had realised that the horse was part of a treacherous plan. Note that
    the snakes had come from the island on which the Greeks were waiting.
227. **teguntur**: lit. 'are hidden', i.e. 'hide themselves'.
228. **tremefacta novus**: *tremefacta* with *pectora* and *novus* with *pavor*. **cunctis**:
    dat. either after *insinuat*, 'worms its way into all', or with *per pectora*,
    'through everyone's heart'. Note the verb chosen by Virgil to describe
    the creeping fear; it reminds us of the snakes.

46

229. **scelus...Laocoonta**: this is an acc. + infin. after *ferunt*, 'that Laocoon had deservedly (*merentem*) paid for his crime'.
230. **ferunt**: 'they say'; the subject is a section of the *cunctis* in line 228. **qui**: note that it is followed by two subjs. and is therefore causal, 'seeing that he'.
231. **laeserit...intorserit**: perf. subjs. 'he damaged'...'he hurled'. **tergo**: dat. after *intorserit*, 'at its back'.
232. **simulacrum**: here refers to the horse. **ducendum**: supply *esse* to be the first part of the ind. statement after *conclamant*, 'that the effigy is to be brought'. **oranda**: supply *esse* to complete the ind. statement.
233. **numina**: with *divae*. Half lines such as this are possibly due to the fact that Virgil did not have time to revise the *Aeneid*.
234. **muros** are the city walls and **moenia** the buildings of the city.
235f. **accingunt**: Virgil is using this intransitively, 'gird themselves', 'equip themselves'. **operi**: 'for the task'. **pedibus...lapsus**: the feet belong to the horse, 'they set beneath (*subiciunt*) its feet gliding wheels (*lapsus rotarum*)'; *lapsus rotarum* lit. 'the glidings of wheels'.
237f. **intendunt**: used here not just for putting something on the horse's neck but drawing it tight. Note that the horse is now described as an engine of war bringing death (*fatalis machina*), and in the next line *feta armis* refers to the armed men in its belly; cf. line 20. **circum**: here adv.
239. **sacra**: i.e. 'sacred songs', probably in honour of Pallas. Virgil's Roman audience would have been reminded of festivals where the young people sang and pulled carts bearing images of the gods. Those scenes of joy were a contrast to this ominous procession.
240. **illa**: i.e. the *machina*, the horse.
241. To add to the tension Virgil makes Aeneas break down as though he cannot face going on with the story. **divum...Ilium**: 'Ilium home of the gods'; *divum* is gen. pl. for *divorum*.
242. **Dardanidum**: gen. pl.
243. **substitit**: 'it halted', 'it stuck'. **utero**: 'from its belly'. **dedere**: for *dederunt*; the subject is *arma*.
244. **caeci furore**: 'blind with frenzy'.
245. **infelix**: n. sg. acc. describing *monstrum*, the horse. Note how Virgil sets *infelix*, a word of ill-omen next to the religious word *sacrata* to highlight the horror of the situation.
246. **fatis futuris**: 'with the fates that were to come'.
247. **ora**: 'her mouth', acc. and the obj. for *aperit*. **dei iussu**: 'on the order of the god'. Cassandra rejected Apollo's love and in revenge Apollo decreed that Cassandra should always prophesy the truth but never be believed.

credita: agrees with *ora* not Cassandra. **Teucris**: dat. used in poetry for *a\ab* + abl., 'by the Trojans'.

248. **delubra**: acc. pl., obj. of *velamus*. **deum**: gen. pl. for *deorum*. **miseri**: with *nos*, 'we, wretches'. **quibus**: dat. pl. 'for whom', refers to *nos*. **esset**: subj. with a causal sense, 'for that was'.

249. **festa**: with *fronde*.

250. **vertitur**: lit. 'is turned', i.e. 'turns'; the pass. is used to make the verb intrans. **Oceano**: abl. 'from the Ocean'. This sentence begins with a spurt in a number of dactyls, but after the abrupt monosyllable *nox* it slows down with a succession of spondees.

252. **fusi**: from *fundo*, 'stretched out'.

253. **conticuere**: for *conticuerunt*. **artus**: acc. pl., 'limbs'.

255. **per...silentia**: 'through the friendly silence', i.e. friendly to the Greeks.

256. **cum**: this is the so-called inverted *cum* = 'when'; the sequence of the actions is: (*ibat*) 'was advancing...(*cum extulerat*) when it had hoisted...(*et laxat*) and he loosens'. **flammas**: 'fire signal'.

257. **deum**: gen. pl. for *deorum*. **defensus**: with *Sinon*. **iniquis**: with *fatis*, 'unfair' to Troy.

258. **inclusos utero**: with *Danaos*, 'shut up in its womb'; again the horse is described as a pregnant animal.

259. **laxat**: used with two object phrases, an example of zeugma; 'he releases the Greeks...loosens the bolts'. The second action explains the first. **Sinon**: the name is kept to the end to emphasise the loathing that Aeneas has for him. **auras**: lit. 'the breezes', i.e. 'the open air'.

260. **laeti**: describes the men named in line 261. Their immediate feeling is one of joy to be out. **cavo robore**: supply *ex*, lit. 'from the hollow oak', i.e. 'from the hollow wood'. Poets very often used a particular wood to mean wood in general; see note to line 112.

262. **lapsi**: partic. of *labor*, 'sliding'.

263. **primus**: the meaning of this adj. is not very clear; since Machaon is not the first out, it cannot mean 'first'; also 'leader' or 'chief' is also possible though Machaon was not one of those commanding a contingent.

264. **doli**: this refers to the horse.

265. **somno vinoque**: 'by sleep and wine', a hendiadys for 'by drunken sleep'.

266. **portis patentibus**: an abl. abs., 'with open gates'.

267. **conscia**: this adj. describes a person involved in a plan or plot.

268. **quo**: abl. referring to *tempus*, 'at which', 'when'. **aegris**: dat., 'weary'.

269. **dono divum**: 'by the gift of the gods'; *divum* for *divorum*.

271. **visus**: supply *est*. **adesse mihi**: lit. 'to be present for me', i.e. 'to be there beside me'. Aeneas now describes his own involvement in the story for

48

the first time. The final i of *mihi* is scanned long here but short in line 274.
272. **raptatus bigis**: Hector had been dragged by Achilles around Troy behind a chariot.
273. **traiectus lora**: this seems to be an unusual case of an acc. retained in the passive (cf. *oculos* l. 210); normally it is the part of the body affected which appears in the acc., 'pierced by thongs'.
274. **qualis**: i.e. 'what a sight'. **quantum**: 'how much', 'how greatly'.
275. **redit**: note the pres. tense; Aeneas visualises Hector again as he comes back from battle. **exuvias indutus**: in this phrase *indutus* is being used like a Greek middle verb, i.e. 'having put on himself', and so an acc. is added, not an abl. **Achilli**: gen. sg. (cf. *Ulixi* l. 7).
276. **Danaum**: gen. pl. for *Danaorum*. **puppibus**: dat. for *in* + acc. **ignes**: note the pl., 'firebrands'.
277. **squalentem...illa**: three objects going with *gerens*. **concretos**: 'matted'.
278. **circum**: with *muros patrios*. **plurima**: 'in very large numbers'. These wounds are those he received when he was dragged around the walls, not those gained in battle which would have been a source of pride not pity.
279. **ultro**: i.e. without waiting to hear what the ghost said. **flens ipse**: 'weeping myself'; the ghost was also weeping, cf. l. 271.
280. **voces**: 'words', as often in poetry.
281. **Teucrum**: gen. pl. for *Teucrorum*.
282. **quae...morae**: *tenuere* for *tenuerunt* supply *te*; a silly question since Aeneas would have known what had happened to Hector; but Virgil knew that dreams are very often unrealistic.
283. **exspectate**: m. voc. sg. agreeing with Hector; 'long awaited'. **ut**: with *aspicimus* 'how', i.e. 'how gladly'.
284. **labores**: 'hardships', 'sufferings', as often in poetry.
285. **defessi**: describes the subject of *aspicimus*, 'we weary ones'. Note the position of *indigna* emphasising the contrast with the next word.
287. **ille**: supply a verb of saying. **vana**: n. pl., obj. of *quaerentem*; 'asking pointless questions'. **moratur**: 'heeds' (Williams).
288. **gemitus**: obj. pl. with *ducens*.
289. **nate dea**: '[you] born of a goddess'; *nate* is m. voc. sg. and *dea* is f. abl. sg.
290. **ruit**: cf. *ruina*; 'is falling in ruins'. **alto...culmine**: 'from its high roof-top'. Note how the rhythm of the sentence matches the meaning.
291. **sat**: subject for *datum*; to *datum* supply *est a te*, 'enough has been given by you', i.e. 'you have given enough'. **dextra**: abl. sg. 'by a right arm', i.e. by deeds of war.
292. **defendi possent**: a pres. unfulfilled condition, 'could be defended'. **hac**:

supply *dextra*; Hector is referring to his own arm. **defensa fuissent**: 'would have been defended'.

293. sacra suosque penates: two objs. of *commendat*; *suos* goes with both nouns.
294. fatorum comites: phrase to describe *hos*, 'as companions of your destiny'. **his**: 'for these'. **moenia**: 'a city', as often in poetry; see note to line 234.
295. magna: adj. more likely in a predic. sense with *quae statues*, 'which you will build up to be great'. **pererrato ponto**: an abl. abs. 'when you have wandered over the sea'.
296f. vittas Vestamque aeternumque ignem: these are the *sacra* mentioned in line 293. The goddess Vesta and the eternal fire were very important to the Romans of Virgil's time; here the poet is suggesting that they were even older than Rome itself. **vittas Vestamque**: possibly a hendiadys, i.e. 'a statue of Vesta [hung with] fillets'.
298. moenia: see note to line 294. These lines (298-301) describe what is going on throughout the city while Aeneas is asleep. **miscentur**: 'is in turmoil' (Williams).
299. secreta: adj. with *domus*, 'remote'; supply *est*.
300. recessit: 'was set back'.
301. clarescunt: 'become distinct'. **armorum**: i.e. 'of the battle'.
303. ascensu supero: 'by climbing I reach '.
304. veluti: the simile which follows compares Aeneas to a shepherd who cannot believe the sound of a fire or a flash flood that is sweeping everything before it. **cum**: 'when'. **furentibus Austris**: an abl. abs., 'when the south winds are raging'.
305. rapidus: much stronger than 'rapid'; it is the adj. version of *rapio*.
306. laeta: 'abundant'.
307. inscius: 'uncomprehending' with *pastor*. **alto**: grammatically with *vertice* but probably should describe *saxi*, 'from the top of a high rock'.
309. fides: either 'proof' or with sarcasm, '[their] trustworthiness'; supply *est*. **Danaum**: gen. pl. for *Danaorum*.
310. ampla: with *domus*, 'the spacious house of Deiphobus'. **dedit ruinam**: lit. 'produced a ruin', i.e. 'fell in ruins'.
311. Volcano superante: an abl. abs. 'as fire overwhelms it'. Volcanus here represents fire; this is a common feature in Latin poetry, cf. Ceres for corn and Bacchus for wine. **proximus**: i.e. 'next door'.
312. Ucalegon: here the name of the owner is used for the house, 'Ucalegon's [house]'. **igni**: abl., 'by the fire'.
313. virum: gen. pl. for *virorum*.
314. amens: a very strong word; i.e. Aeneas does not know what he is doing. **nec sat rationis**: supply *est*, lit. 'nor is there enough reason', i.e. he has

not thought out what he is going to do with his weapons; he has no plan in mind.

315. glomerare, concurrere: both depend on *ardent animi*. **manum**: here 'a band'. **bello**: dat. 'for war'.

316. ardent animi: *animi* is a pl. for sg. 'my mind is fired up to...'. Note how the raging fire in Troy is mirrored by the state of Aeneas' mind. His mind is out of control (*furor ira)* and there is no way of stopping him (*praecipitat*).

317. succurrit: an impers. verb, 'it occurs to me', which is followed by an acc. and infin., *pulchrum* + *esse* (supplied). **mori in armis**: a glorious death in battle was the aim of all heroic warriors; Homer's epic poem the *Iliad*, which also deals with the siege of Troy, portrays such warriors seeking honour and glory in war. Aeneas' immediate reaction to the destruction of his country is to fall back on old patterns of behaviour.

318. telis: abl. with *elapsus* 'having escaped from...'. **Achivum**: gen. pl. for *Achivorum*. **Panthus**: final vowel is long.

319. The poet seems to give Panthus his full, official title. **arcisque Phoebique**: i.e. of the temple of Phoebus on the citadel.

320. sacra: n. pl. obj. of *trahit*, 'sacred objects'. **victos deos**: gods were thought to protect their people; clearly the gods of the Trojans have been conquered along with the Trojans. Panthus is visualised as carrying small statues. The two sets of objects presumably were in one hand which left the other free for his *nepotem*.

321. trahit: this verb is used with all three objects; with *sacra* and *deos* it must have the sense of *portat*. **amens**: cf. line 314. **cursu**: 'by running'. **limina**: the doorway here is that of Anchises' house through which Aeneas himself is rushing.

322. quo loco: for *in quo loco*. **summa res**: 'the most important action', i.e. the decisive fighting; supply *est*. **quam...arcem**: 'what stronghold have we seized'; *prendimus* is probably perf.

323. gemitu: to be taken after *cum* which here is 'when'.

324. venit: perf. here as scansion makes clear. **summa**: 'final'. The rhythm and sound of this line add to the despair of the speaker.

325. fuimus: 'we have been' and are no more; *fuit* has the same sense. Note also the emphatic repetition of this verb.

326. Argos: acc. pl. 'to Argos'; i.e. all the power and glory of Troy have now gone to Argos, the centre of Agamemnon's kingdom.

328. arduus: describes *equus*. Note the alliteration in this line.

329. incendia miscet: lit. 'mixes fires', i.e. 'throws firebrands in all directions'.

330. insultans: note the emphatic position to add weight to this word. **alii**: with *alii* in line 332, 'some...others'. **bipatentibus**: *bi-* indicates that it is 'double' gates that are lying open.

331. **quot milia**: 'as many thousands as'. **venere**: for *venerunt*.

332. **obsedere**: for *obsederunt*. **angusta viarum**: lit. 'the narrows of the streets', i.e. either 'the narrow streets' or 'the narrow parts of the streets'. **telis oppositis**: an abl. abs. 'with weapons set before them'.

333. **stat**: note the monosyllable at the start, adding a feeling of solidity. **acies ferri**: either 'a line of steel' using *acies* in the sense of a battle line, or 'an edge of steel' using it in the sense of a cutting edge.

334. **stricta**: agrees with *acies* but really describes *ferri*. **parata neci**: i.e. ready to inflict death. **primi**: describes *vigiles*.

335. **caeco Marte**: 'with aimless warfare'.

336. **talibus...divum**: two phrases giving reasons for Aeneas' sudden action; the abl. endings of *dictis* and *numine* = 'as a result of'. **divum**: for *divorum*.

337. **feror**: lit. 'I am borne', i.e. 'I rush'. **quo**: 'whither'. **tristis Erinys**: 'the grim Fury', a goddess that represented a force driving someone to destruction.

338. **quo**: see l. 337. **aethera**: a so-called Greek acc. sg.

339. **socios**: 'as companions', cf. *comites* in line 294.

340. **oblati**: referring to Rhipeus and Epytus; the passive of *offero* means 'I appear'.

341. **adglomerant**: this verb requires an obj.; supply *se* from line 339.

343. **amore Cassandrae**: 'with love for Cassandra'; *Cassandrae* is an objective gen.

344. **gener**: this is what Coroebus hoped to be, 'as his would-be son-in-law'.

345. **qui**: this is followed by *audierit*, a perf. subj., and has a causal sense, 'since he'. **furentis**: a mad frenzy was expected in prophets; it was thought to be the sign of divine inspiration.

346. **audierit**: 'heeded' rather than 'heard'.

347. **quos confertos audere vidi**: 'I saw that they (*quos*) were closely packed (*confertos*) and had the courage (*audere*) for battle'; note that it is *audere* not *audire*.

348. **super his**: *super* is an adv., 'in addition'; supply *verbis* to *his*. Aeneas wishes to rouse their fighting spirit still further. **fortissima frustra**: Aeneas means that all their brave actions so far have been in vain.

349f. **si vobis cupido**: 'if your desire'. **audendi extrema**: describing *cupido*; lit. 'of daring the ultimate'. **certa sequi**: *certa* describes *cupido*; supply *est* and *me*, 'is set to follow me'. **quae...fortuna**: an ind. quest. after *videtis*; 'what is the fate of [our] affairs'. Aeneas is indicating that all is now lost; cf. *frustra* in line 348.

351. **omnes**: with *di*. **excessere**: for *excesserunt*. **adytis...relictis**: an abl. abs. It

was commonly believed that the gods and goddesses left their temples when a city or town was doomed.

352. **quibus**: 'by whom', i.e. 'with whose help'.

353. **moriamur...ruamus**: the first verb is like a battle cry; the rest is how this is to be achieved, for death in battle brought glory to a warrior. **arma**: 'battle' or 'fighting'.

354. **salus**: supply *est*. Behind this strange statement lies the idea that to be conquered and survive possibly meant suffering degradation, for example, living as a slave. **victis**: dat., 'for the vanquished'.

355. **additus**: supply *est*. **lupi ceu**: take *ceu* first.

356f. **raptores**: here an adj. with *lupi*, 'ravening'. **improba**: with *rabies ventris*, lit. 'an uncontrollable rage of the belly', i.e. 'an uncontrollable hunger'.

357. **exegit caecos**: *caecos* describes *quos*; 'has driven out blindly'. The *ex-* suggests that they have been forced out of their safe lairs.

358. **siccis**: i.e. needing to be moistened by blood and therefore 'thirsty'.

359f. **mediae urbis**: a gen. phrase; translate with *iter* as 'a course towards the middle of the city'.

360. **atra**: with *nox*. **cava**: abl. sg. with *umbra*, 'enfolding'.

361f. **quis explicet...aut possit**: note the pres. subj., 'who would unfold...or could'. The second *quis* in place of *et* is a rhetorical device to make the question more forceful. Note the bitterness in the alliteration of *f*. **fando**: abl. of the gerund of *for*; lit. 'by speaking', i.e. 'in speech'. **labores**: 'sufferings'; note the second alliteration here.

363. **ruit**: this verb is connected to *ruina*, 'is falling in ruins'.

364. **plurima**: with *inertia corpora*.

366. **soli**: with *Teucri*, 'not only the Trojans'.

367. **quondam**: 'from time to time'. **victis**: dat. pl. with *in praecordia*, 'into the hearts of the vanquished'. Note the alliteration of *v* to give more force to the thought of a renewed courage; here we have the irony of courage restored to the vanquished and death coming to the victors. Virgil deliberately chooses the connected words *victis* and *victores*.

369. **luctus**: supply *est*. **pavor**: final syllable is long here before the caesura; cf. *obruimur* (l. 411). **plurima imago**: i.e. 'very many forms'.

370f. **primus**: with *Danaum*. **Danaum**: for *Danaorum*. **se offert**: cf. note to line 340, i.e. 'meets us'. **magna...caterva**: an abl. abs. **Androgeos**: a Gk. nom. sg.; cf. also line 392. **socia**: Androgeos thought Aeneas' men were allies; supply *esse*.

372. **ultro**: cf. notes to lines 145 and 193.

373f. **quae...segnities**: a compressed sentence; lit. 'what [is] the so dilatory sluggishness [that] delays you?' Put it into a more colloquial version;

perhaps *tam* should be ignored. **alii...vos**: note the contrast. **rapiunt feruntque**: this is clearly a variant on the normal phrase for plundering, *fero et ago*.

375. **nunc primum**: 'now for the first time'.
377. **fida satis**: 'sufficiently trustworthy' describing *responsa*. **delapsus**: = *se delapsum esse*; this imitates a construction in Greek where verbs of realisation are following by a participle.
378. **retroque...repressit**: i.e. he stopped speaking and backed off at the same time.
379. **veluti qui**: this introduces a simile and should be translated first; 'just like a man who'. **aspris sentibus**: abl. phrase (*aspris* for *asperis*) explaining why the snake was not seen, lit. 'by', i.e. 'because of'.
380. **nitens**: 'treading on it' (Williams); this word with its two long syllables emphasises the pressure and contrasts with the short syllables that follow describing the sudden reaction. **refugit**: perf. here, supply *eum* (the snake) as an obj.
381. **attollentem...tumentem**: describe *eum* supplied to line 380. **colla**: so-called acc. of respect, going with *tumentem* and defining the place affected, 'swelling in his neck'.
382. **haud secus**: lit. 'not otherwise', i.e. 'just so'; this brings us back to the story. **abibat**: 'was trying to get away'.
383. **circumfundimur**: pass. used for the reflexive phrase *nos circumfundimus*, i.e. 'we surround [them]'.
384. **ignarosque loci**: the Greeks being invaders did not know their way about the city. **captos**: 'gripped'.
385. **aspirat**: lit. 'breathes on', i.e. 'smiles on' (Williams); *Fortuna* is viewed here as a following wind.
386. **hic**: referring to time not place, 'at this point'. **successu animisque**: a compressed phrase with *exsultans* but really containing two different ideas, 'with success and [in] high spirits'.
387. **qua**: 'in which direction', 'where'; also in l. 388.
388. **ostendit se**: subject of this is *fortuna* repeated from previous verb. **dextra**: nom. here with *fortuna*, as the scansion proves.
389. **mutemus**: note the subj. 'let us change'; like *sequamur* above and *aptemus* (l. 390). **Danaum**: gen pl. for *Danaorum*. **insignia**: probably the designs on the shields.
390. **dolus...virtus**: the *an* shows that this is a compressed double question, *utrum dolus sit an virtus*, depending on *requirat* which is also in the subj.; 'who would ask whether it is trickery or bravery in [the case of] an enemy?' The short clipped phrases here and in line 391 add to the urgency

54

of Coroebus' words.
391. **deinde**: postponed here; take as first word in sentence.
392. **Androgeo**: a Gk. genitive; cf. line 371. **clipeique...decorum**: 'the beautiful design of the shield', i.e. 'the shield with its beautiful design'.
393. **induitur**: pass. in a reflexive sense; 'he puts on [himself]'. See also line 275.
395. **laeta**: f. nom. sg. adj. with *iuventus*; but translate as 'happily'.
396. **haud...nostro**: by changing armour these Trojans also change their protecting gods.
397. **congressi**: refers to meeting groups of the enemy, 'having engaged'.
398. **conserimus**: with *proelia* as its obj. 'we join battles'. **Danaum**: cf. line 389. **Orco**: dat. for *ad Orcum*; cf. *neci* l. 85.
399. **cursu**: 'by running'; see also l. 321.
400. **fida**: the Greeks could trust the shores because their ships were there and they knew them, unlike the streets of the city. **pars**: a monosyllabic substitute for *alii*.
401. **conduntur**: pass. in a reflexive sense, 'they hide [themselves]'.
402. **heu...divis**: supply *est* with *fas*, *nihil* is an adv. here; lit. 'alas, it is right (*fas est*) that anyone (*quemquam*) should trust the unwilling gods in nothing', i.e. 'it is right that no one should trust the gods when they are unwilling in anything'. The main reason for this outburst comes in the next line.
403. **Priameia virgo**: 'Priam's maiden daughter'; her name comes in line 404. **passis**: adj. with *crinibus*.
404. **templo adytisque**: the *templum* was the whole building and the *adytum* the innermost and most sacred shrine; here both words are used to increase the sense of horror at the sacrilege.
405. **tendens**: 'directing'; she is looking for help.
406. **lumina**: the repeat of this word heightens the pathos of the scene. Normally Romans stretched out their hands in prayer; Cassandra could only use her eyes.
407. **furiata mente**: 'with his frenzied state of mind'.
408. **medium**: with *agmen*. **sese**: = *se*. **periturus**: i.e. 'to his death'; the partic. here describes the inevitable consequence of his action.
409. **densis armis**: 'with close-packed arms'.
410. **delubri**: i.e 'of Minerva's temple', cf. line 404.
411. **nostrorum**: with *telis*, 'by the weapons of our own men'. Aeneas and his band are now dressed as Greeks and so come under attack from Trojan defenders. **obruimur**: the final syll. of this is long coming before the caesura; cf. *pavor* line 369.
412. **armorum...iubarum**: note the chiastic order of the words; 'from the

55

appearance of the armour and from mistaking the Greek crests'.

413. ereptae...ira: *ira* is abl., and *ereptae virginis* an object. gen. phrase; lit. 'with anger at the snatched girl', i.e. 'in anger at the snatching of the girl'. Possibly *gemitu* and *ira* are a hendiadys, 'with a groan of anger at'. Evidently Cassandra was rescued by those with Aeneas.

415. gemini Atridae: 'the twin sons of Atreus'. They are included here probably because in the legendary account Cassandra became a slave-girl of Agamemnon.

416. ceu: this introduces a simile and should go first. **adversi:** describing *venti*, 'against one another'. **rupto turbine:** an abl. abs., 'when a tornado has broken out'.

418. equis: with *Eois* forms an abl. phrase after *laetus*, 'happy with his eastern horses'. **stridunt...saevitque:** Note the alliteration of *s* to suggest the rushing winds. Winds were often portrayed in words and pictures as chariots drawn by horses. **tridenti:** abl. sg.; this weapon is usually wielded by Neptune.

419. imo fundo: abl. phrase, supply *ab/ex*; 'from its lowest depth'.

420. illi...si quos: lit. 'those...if any', i.e. 'any whom'; *quos* comes from the indefinite *quis* commonly used after *si*. These are Greeks whom Aeneas and his band have been defeating. **obscura nocte:** supply *in.*

421. insidiis: 'by our strategem'. **tota urbe:** abl. phrase to mark the locality, 'over the whole city'.

422. apparent: note how the position of this word, separated from its subject, emphasises the suddenness of their appearance.

mentita tela: lit. 'lying weapons'; i.e. though they were Greek weapons they were held in fact by Trojans.

423. ora: lit. 'mouths', i.e. 'speech'. **sono:** probably abl., 'by its sound'. **discordia:** the Greeks notice that the speech of Aeneas' band does not match the shields and armour they have. **signant:** 'they note'.

425. dextra: abl. sg. **divae armipotentis:** i.e. Pallas, known to the Greeks as Athene; statues of Athene normally show her fully armed like a warrior. This phrase goes with *ad aram*.

426. iustissimus unus: with *qui...Teucris*, i.e. 'the most just of all'.

427. servantissimus: a superl. adj. from the verb *servo*; 'the most observant'. **aequi:** n. gen. sg. of the adj. used here as a noun going with *servantissimus*, 'of what is fair'.

428. dis...visum: a bitter comment from the speaker; supply *est* to *visum*, 'it appeared differently to the gods'. Since Rhipeus was such an honourable person, it might be supposed that the gods would have kept him safe.

429. a sociis: i.e. they were killed by Trojans. **te tua:** note the alliteration to emphasise the bitterness again felt by the speaker. **te**: with *labentem*. **tua plurima**: with *pietas*; this phrase is the first subject. **Panthu**: voc. sg. of *Panthus* (cf. l. 319).

430. The *infula* was a headband entwined with wool, worn by priests; it was expected that a priest in his religious garments would be treated with respect.

431. Iliaci...meorum: *cineres* and *flamma* are voc., 'you ashes of Troy and final flame of my people'.

432f. testor: supply *me* with *vitavisse* to form an acc. + infin., 'I call [you] to witness that I avoided'. **tela, vices**: both obj. of *vitavisse*.

433. vices Danaum: following Williams, I take these together; *Danaum* for *Danaorum*, 'answering blows of the Greeks'. **si...fuissent**: supply *mihi* or *mea*, 'if it had been my fate'.

434. caderem: to die in battle was the most glorious fate for a warrior. **meruisse**: supply *me* to form a second acc. + infin. after *testor*, 'that I would have deserved it '. **manu**: i.e. 'by my deeds'.

435. aevo: with *gravior*, 'rather ponderous through age'.

436. et: 'also'. **Vlixi**: lit. 'of Ulysses', i.e. 'inflicted by Ulysses'.

437. vocati: supply *sumus*. **clamore**: 'by shouting'.

438f. ingentem pugnam: obj. of *cernimus* in line 441. **ceu**: 'as if'. **cetera... forent**: *forent* for *essent*, lit. 'as if the rest of the battles existed nowhere', i.e. 'as if there were no battles anywhere else'.

439. nulli morerentur: also after *ceu*, 'and none were dying'.

440. Martem indomitum: i.e. unrestrained fighting. **tecta**: 'buildings'.

441. acta testudine: 'by an advancing (*acta*) tortoise formation'; the *testudo* was a body of Roman soldiers who advanced holding their shields over themselves for protection.

442. parietibus: the first syllable is scanned long with the *i* treated as a consonant. **postes sub ipsos**: 'close to the very doors'.

443. nituntur gradibus: 'they struggle up the rungs'. **clipeos**: obj. of *obiciunt*. **sinistris**: with *protecti*. **ad tela**: 'against the missiles'.

444. protecti: this is probably intended in a reflexive sense, 'protecting themselves'; cf. *teguntur* line 227.

445. contra: adv. here.

446. his: with *telis*. **se**: obj. with *defendere*. **quando**: 'since'. **ultima**: perhaps *adesse* should be supplied.

447. extrema in morte: i.e. 'at the point of death'.

448. decora: n. pl. adj. here used as a noun, 'ornaments'. The reference is to family heirlooms.

449. imas: with *fores*, lit. 'lowest', i.e. 'down below'; in contrast to those on the roof tops.

450. obsedere: for *obsederunt,* 'they blockaded'. **servant:** 'they guard'.

451. instaurati animi: supply *sunt* and *mei,* 'my courage was renewed to...'; this phrase is followed by the infins.

452. Note the alliteration of *v* in this line.

453f. caecae: lit. 'blind', i.e. 'concealed'. **pervius usus tectorum inter se:** *usus* is a noun and *pervius* an adj.; but in translation it is easier to reverse these, *tectorum inter se,* lit. 'of buildings among themselves', i.e. 'an habitually used passageway from building to building'. It becomes clear in lines 455-7 that Hector and Andromache live in part of Priam's palace and the passageway was for them to go to and fro.

454f. postes...tergo: 'a door unnoticed in the rear'; *relinquo* can be used of passing over something or leaving something unnoticed.

455. infelix: with *Andromache.* **qua:** 'by which', referring to *postes.* **se:** with *ferre.* **regna:** pl. for sg. as often in poetry, 'the kingdom'.

456. ferre se: 'to take herself'.

457. ad soceros: 'to her parents-in-law'. **Astyanacta:** Gk. acc. sg. **trahebat:** the poet chose this word to portray a child being pulled along by his mother and barely able to keep up with her.

458. evado: we may presume that Aeneas used the *postes a tergo* to enter the palace; 'I emerge out onto *(ad)*'. **summi...culminis:** 'the summit *(fastigia)* of the highest roof'.

459. manu: i.e. 'with might and main', not just 'by hand'.

460f. turrim: obj. of three verbs: *adgressi, convellimus* and *impulimus.* **in praecipiti:** 'at the edge'. **sub astra eductam:** 'built up to the stars'. **summis:** with *tectis,* 'on the top of the roof'.

461. unde: refers to the tower. **videri:** after *solitae,* 'to be seen'.

462. Danaum: for *Danaorum.* **solitae:** supply *sunt* ; this verb has three subjects: *Troia, naves* and *castra.* It is f. and pl. to agree with the nearest.

463f. ferro: lit. 'with iron', i.e. 'with axes'. **circum:** adv. 'all around'. **qua:** 'where'. **summa:** with *tabulata,* lit. 'highest' i.e. 'top'. **labantes iuncturas:** 'joints that were giving way'. **dabant:** 'offered'. **altis sedibus:** 'from its high base'.

465. ea: 'it', referring to the tower. Note how the poet places the *-que* immediately before a break suggesting that the tower swayed for a moment on the edge before it fell.

466. Danaum: for *Danaorum.*

470. telis et luce aena: a hendiadys with *coruscus*; 'with weapons and a gleam of bronze', i.e. 'with gleaming weapons of bronze'.

471. in lucem: *lucem* is the link between the story and the simile; this phrase goes with *convolvit*. **mala gramina**: obj. with *pastus* in a reflexive sense, 'having feasted itself (*pastus*) on noxious herbs'.

472. **quem**: this word should be translated first. **tumidum**: 'swollen [with food]'.

473. **positis**: i.e. 'shed', with *exuviis* in an abl. abs.. **iuventa**: abl. sg. with *nitidus*, 'glistening in its youth'.

475. **arduus ad solem**: 'rearing up to the sun'. **ore**: supply *ex*. **trisulcis**: lit. 'triple forked'; this is a poetic exaggeration, i.e. 'forked'.

476. **una**: adv., also in line 477.

479. **ipse**: i.e. Pyrrhus. **correpta dura**: scansion makes clear that *correpta* is abl. sg. with *bipenni* but *dura* n. pl. 'unyielding' with *limina* 'doors'.

480. **perrumpit...vellit**: both pres. tenses 'is trying to...' in contrast to *cavavit* and *dedit* which follow. **a cardine**: 'from their socket'; ancient doors opened and shut by turning in a socket.

481. **excisa trabe**: abl. abs., lit. 'a panel cut out', i.e. 'after he cut out a panel'.

482. **ingentem...fenestram**: 'gave it a huge window with a wide opening'.

483. **domus intus**: 'the house within'. In lines 483-5 Virgil describes the almost sacred privacy of the royal palace being ruthlessly violated. Note the emphatic repetition of *apparet...apparent*.

484. **penetralia**: commonly used of the most sacred parts of a temple; here 'the inner rooms'.

485. **vident**: the subject of this is presumably Priam and his family.

486. **domus interior**: i.e. 'the interior part of the house'.

487f. **miscetur**: 'is in turmoil'. **penitusque**: 'and deep within'. **plangoribus ululant**: 'echo with the shrieks of lamentation'.

488. **aurea**: in contrast to the dreadful horrors taking place on earth.

489. **tectis**: abl. of place with *ingentibus*, 'in the huge rooms'.

491. **vi patria**: *patria* is an adj. here, 'with his father's violence'. Achilles who had recently killed Hector was the father of Pyrrhus.

492. **ariete**: the *i* is a consonant here and so the word scans as a dactyl. **ariete crebro**: 'with the frequent [assaults of the] battering ram'.

493. **emoti cardine**: 'wrenched from their socket'; cf. note to line 480.

494. **fit via vi**: a striking phrase emphasising the sudden rush of the attackers as they pour in through the smashed doors. **rumpunt aditus**: subject is *Danai immissi*, 'they force their entry'; *aditus* is an obj. pl.

495. **immissi**: lit. 'having been let loose' or 'hurled at', i.e. 'charging'. **milite**: a collective noun, 'with soldiery'.

496. **non sic**: lit. 'not thus', i.e. 'not with such violence'. **aggeribus ruptis**: an abl. abs. **cum**: 'whenever', to be taken first.

497. **gurgite**: 'with its raging water'.

498. fertur: 'it rushes'. **furens cumulo**: 'raging with its heaped up mass'. Note the double alliteration of *f* and *c*.

499f. trahit: i.e. 'sweeps away'. **furentem caede**: 'raging with slaughter'; this phrase ties the simile into the story.

500. Neoptolemum: another name for Pyrrhus.

501. Note the repetition of *vidi* giving a vivid force to the description. **nurus**: acc. pl.; Priam and Hecuba were said to have had fifty sons and fifty daughters and since the sons were married, *nurus* refers to both daughters and daughters-in-law. **per**: 'among'.

502. quos: refers to *ignes*; take *ignes* first as obj. of *foedantem*.

504f. auro spoliisque superbi: *auro spoliisque* probably a hendiadys, 'proud with spoils of gold'; note the alliteration and the word order. The doorposts used to be adorned with booty taken in war but their pride was crushed so swiftly. **procubuere**: for *procubuerunt*. **qua**: adv. The description ends here in a scene of utter desolation.

506. The word order for translation is : *forsitan et requiras quae fuerint fata Priami*. **requiras**: note the subj. as is usual after *forsitan*. **et**: 'also'. **fuerint**: subj. for ind. question. Virgil places *Priami* early in the line as he is the point of the enquiry. This line is addressed first to Dido, then to any listener or reader.

507. uti: = *ut*, 'when'; take this first. **convulsa**: with *limina*.

508. penetralibus hostem: The choice and position of the words increases the sense of horror; *penetralia* is often used to describe sacred and secret places. **hostem**: i.e. Pyrrhus.

509f. diu: with *desueta*. **senior**: = *senex*. **arma circumdat umeris**: 'puts his armour around his shoulders'. **aevo**: with *trementibus*.

511. cingitur: in a reflexive sense, 'girds on [himself]'; cf. line 275. **fertur**: 'he rushes', cf. line 498. **moriturus**: see note on *periturus* (l. 408). Virgil emphasises the pointless action of Priamus with words like *trementibus aevo, nequiquam* and *inutile*.

512. Priam's palace is described as though it was a normal Roman house with a portion open to the sky. Note also *penates* in line 514.

513. iuxta: adv. 'next to it'.

514. incumbens : lit. 'leaning on' + dat., i.e. 'overhanging'. **umbra complexa**: *complexa* describing *laurus*; *umbra* is abl. sg. 'embracing with its shade'.

515. nequiquam: with *sedebant* in line 517; cf. note to line 511. **circum**: here placed after its noun. **altaria**: here pl. for sg.

516. praecipites: describing *columbae*, 'driven headlong'. **ceu**: 'like', take this first to introduce the simile.

517. condensae: 'huddled together'. **divum**: gen. pl. for *divorum*.

518. sumptis iuvenalibus armis: abl. abs. 'having taken up the arms of his youth'; see lines 509-510.

519. ut vidit: 'when she saw', take this phrase before line 518. **mens**: 'intention', 'purpose'.

520. impulit: supply *te* as obj. **cingi**: pres. pass. infin. in a reflexive sense, 'to gird yourself'; cf. *cingitur* line 511. **aut**: as Williams points out, this word introduces another question and not an alternative to the first.

521. auxilio, defensoribus: both abl. after *eget*. **istis**: *iste* is used to mean 'that of yours', perhaps here 'defenders like you'.

522. tempus: 'the situation'. **non, si...Hector**: Servius, an ancient commentator, thought that *non* was all that is left of the second part of the 'if' sentence. Supply *Troiam servare posset*; *adforet* = *adesset*, 'even if my Hector himself were here now, [he would] not [be able to save Troy]'.

523. tandem: expressing Hecuba's exasperation at Priam's silly behaviour, 'finally'. **omnes**: i.e. *nos omnes*.

524. moriere: for *morieris*. **simul**: i.e. 'along with us'. **effata**: 'having spoken', referring to Hecuba, the subject. Virgil is marking the end of Hecuba's speech; remember that the poem was written to be read aloud. **recepit**: supply *eum* as obj.

525. sese: for *se*.

526. Ecce: to mark a sudden change of topic. **elapsus de**: 'having escaped from'. **caede Pyrrhi**: 'the slaughter [wrought by] Pyrrhus'; *Pyrrhi* is a subject. gen.

527. natorum: a noun here.

528. porticibus longis: abl., 'down the long colonnades'. **fugit**: pres. as scansion shows.

529. saucius: note how Virgil put this at the end to give it emphasis. **infesto vulnere**: the related verb *infenso* means to act in a threatening and hostile manner, 'with a threatening weapon'; *vulnus*, as Williams points out, is used by Virgil for the weapon that causes the wound; cf. *Aen.* VII 533.

530. iam iamque: emphasising how close Pyrrhus is to grabbing him. **premit**: 'presses upon him'. **hasta**: abl.

531. ut: 'when'. **ante**: with *oculos et ora*. **evasit**: 'he emerged', i.e. out of the colonnades and halls of the palace.

532. concidit: note the position; Polites immediately collapsed.

533. hic: adv. of time here. **tenetur**: 'is hemmed in' (Page), i.e. the enemy was closing in.

534. voci iraeque: a hendiadys, i.e. 'angry words'.

535. at: often used to introduce curses. **tibi**: with *di persolvant*, 'may the gods pay to you'; note the subj. for a wish and the emphatic position of *tibi*.

536. qua: f. sg. nom. of *quis* with *si pietas*, 'if any justice'. **pietas**: Priam thinks that the gods ought to show *pietas* to him and his family, since they have always honoured the gods. **caelo**: abl. supply *in*, 'in heaven', i.e. among the gods.

538. qui: the antecedent for this is *tibi* (l. 535), 'you who'. **nati**: gen. sg. with *letum*. **coram**: adv. here, 'in front of me'.

539. foedasti: for *foedavisti*. **patrios vultus**: 'a father's sight'; *vultus* acc. pl. Note the use of alliterative *f* in this line to emphasise Priam's bitterness.

540f. ille: with *Achilles*, 'that [famous] Achilles'. **non fuit talis**: 'was not so', i.e. did not behave like that. **satum...mentiris**: supply *esse* to *satum*; 'from whom (*quo*) you falsely say (*mentiris*) that you were produced (*te satum esse*)'. **in hoste**: 'in the case of his enemy'.

542. erubuit: lit. 'he blushed', i.e. 'he respected'. **sepulcro**: 'for burial'. Priam had already been as a suppliant to Achilles to beg for the corpse of his son Hector.

544. fatus: supply *est*, perf. of *for*. **senior**: see line 509. **ictu**: 'force'.

545. quod: 'which', referring to *telum*. **rauco**: with *aere*, lit. 'harshly sounding', i.e. 'echoing'. **repulsum**: supply *est*.

546. summo: with *umbone*, 'from the surface of the boss' (Williams).

547. cui Pyrrhus: supply *dixit*. **nuntius**: 'as a messenger'.

548. Pelidae genitori: 'to my father Pelides'; *Pelides* is a patronymic, referring to Achilles as son of Peleus. **illi**: dat. sg., 'to him'.

549. degenerem: supply *esse* to complete the acc. + infin. **memento**: sg. imperat. of *memini*, with *narrare*, 'remember to relate'.

550f. morere: sg. imperat. of *morior*. **ipsa**: this was put in by Virgil to emphasise the shocking nature of what is about to happen. **trementem, lapsantem**: both agree with *eum* (Priam) which has to be supplied as the obj. of *traxit*.

552. laeva, dextra: both abl. sg.. **coruscum**: note the position of this; it is flashing when it is raised. By the end of the sentence, when we meet *ensem*, it is buried.

553. lateri: dat. sg. for *in latus*. **tenus**: comes after its noun/pronoun.

554. haec: supply *erat*. **finis**: here f. as it is occasionally.

555f. tulit: with *illum*, 'carried him off'. **videntem**: with *illum*, 'as he saw'. **Troiam incensam et prolapsa Pergama**: this phrase is obj. of *videntem*. **tot**: with *populis terrisque* (abl.); translate with *superbum*, i.e. 'proud with'.

557f. litore: for *in litore*. The final sentence is one of complete despair and desolation; everything was now lost – the power and wealth of the kingdom were gone, the city was a blazing ruin and the king an unidentifiable corpse left on the shore.

559. tum primum: Virgil is marking the first moment that Aeneas realises all is lost. He is now no longer concerned about the city but about his family.

560. **subiit**: this verb is often used of thoughts, ideas, feelings and even visions coming into someone's mind. **genitoris**: supply *mei*.

561. **ut**: here, 'when'. **aequaevum**: 'of the same age [as him]'; the sight of the dying Priam triggered off the thoughts of his father.

563. **direpta domus**: his house had not really been plundered; he began to fear that perhaps it had been. **casus**: nom. sg. here.

564. **quae**: introducing an ind. quest., note the subj. *sit*; translate *lustro* first. **copia**: here in the sg., 'force'. **me circum**: 'around me'.

565f. **deseruere**: for *deseruerunt*, supply *me*. **saltu**: lit. 'with a leap'; with *misere* for *miserunt* and *corpora*, 'they leapt'. **aegra**: with *corpora* supplied from previous line, 'fainting' or 'exhausted'. **dedere**: for *dederunt*; 'surrendered'.

567. **super**: with *eram* forming a compound verb; such a splitting is called tmesis. **cum**: here 'when'; an example of so-called inverted *cum*.

568. **servantem**: partic., like *tacitam* and *latentem* describing *Tyndarida*, 'keeping close to', followed by *limina Vestae*.

569. **Tyndarida**: patronymic, so-called Gk. acc. sg., 'daughter of Tyndareus' (Helen). **clara**: here 'bright'.

570. **erranti, ferenti**: supply *mihi*. **oculos ferenti**: i.e. 'casting glances'. **per cuncta**: i.e. 'all over the place'. Aeneas is peering down from the roof; he does not come down until line 632.

571f. **illa sibi**: with *praemetuens* (line 573), 'she fearing for herself'; *prae*- 'beforehand', because she does not really know how they will react to her. **infestos Teucros**: the first of three objs. of *praemetuens*; the others are *poenas* and *iras*. **Danaum**: for *Danaorum*. **coniugis**: her husband was Menelaus. **iras**: note the pl., probably 'angry outbursts'.

573. **Troiae...Erinys**: a phrase describing Helen; see also line 337; **communis**: because she was bringing destruction both to Greece (*patriae*) and Troy.

574. **sese**: = *se*. **aris**: abl. i.e. 'at the altars'. **invisa**: either 'hated' or 'unseen', perhaps intentionally both.

575. **animo**: abl., 'from my heart'. **exarsere**: for *exarserunt*. **ira**: 'a passion'. **subit**: see line 560. **cadentem**: with *patriam*.

576. **ulcisci**: infin. after *ira subit*, 'a passion comes over me to avenge'. **sceleratas poenas**: 'wicked vengeance' (cf. Williams); Aeneas is here thinking back and realises it would have been a wicked act to have killed a woman at an altar. If he had done so he would have been no better than Pyrrhus; see line 550.

577. **scilicet**: introducing a bitter, cynical remark, 'no doubt'; the futs. and fut. perfs. indicate a feeling of 'will all these things happen and I do nothing about it?'. **haec**: sg. f. nom. 'this woman'. **incolumis**: with *haec*.

578. parto...triumpho: abl. abs., *parto* from *pario*, 'gaining a triumph'. Virgil describes Helen's return to Greece as though it was the return of a victorious general to Rome. **regina**: 'as a queen'.

579. coniugium: here Virgil uses the abstract noun 'marriage' for the concrete one 'husband'.

580. Iliadum: 'of Trojan women'. **turba, ministris**: both abl. after *comitata* from *comitor*, 'accompanied', which is nom. sg.

581. occiderit: 'will have fallen', a fut. perf. like *arserit* and *sudarit*. **igni**: old abl. sg.

582. sudarit: for *sudaverit*, lit. 'will have sweated', i.e. 'will have been drenched'. The use of this particular verb reminds the reader that the blood came from a human body and was warm.

583. namque: = *nam*. **nomen**: here 'fame' or 'renown'.

584. feminea...poena: 'in a woman's punishment'. The punishment here is the killing of Helen. **victoria**: '[such a] conquest'.

585. exstinxisse, sumpsisse: both perf. infins. after *laudabor* as though it is a verb of saying, 'I will be praised for having ...'. **nefas**: a neuter noun to refer to the hated Helen.

586. explesse: shortened form of *explevisse* the perf. infin. **iuvabit**: supply *me*, 'it will please me to have...'.

587. flammae: gen. sg.; 'with flame', i.e. a burning fury. Verbs of filling or satisfying are often followed by the gen. for 'with'. **satiasse**: shortened form of *satiavisse*. **meorum**: 'of my people'.

588. ferebar: 'I was rushing off'; the passive of *fero* is often used for very swift movement, cf. lines 511 and 725. Aeneas gives way to his rage and rushes off to take vengeance on Helen.

589f. cum: so-called inverted *cum*, 'when'. **mihi se**: with *obtulit alma parens videndam*, 'my kindly parent presented herself to me to be seen'. **oculis**: dat. pl., 'to my eyes'. **clara**: f. nom. sg. describing *alma parens*. **pura**: 'clear', abl. sg. with *luce*.

591f. confessa: supply *se* and translate as a pres. partic., 'making herself known'. **qualis...quanta**: lit. 'in what form...in what size' with *solet videri*, referring to her appearance and height. Usually the gods took on a human form, but here Aeneas is privileged to see his mother as she appeared to the other gods and goddesses. **dextra**: abl. sg. **prehensum**: describing *me* supplied as obj. of *continuit*.

593. haec: n. pl. acc., 'these words'. **insuper**: adv.

594. quis: adj. with *tantus dolor*, 'what [is] the so great resentment [that]...'.

595. quid: here 'why'. **nostri tibi cura**: *nostri* for *mei*, *tibi* in a possessive sense, 'your regard for me'.

596. non...ubi: a direct and then ind. quest., 'will you not see first where...'.
597. liqueris: perf. subj. for ind. quest. **superet**: pres. subj., 'survives'. **-ne**: introducing a second question, 'and whether'.
598. quos omnes: acc. phrase after *circum*, 'around all of whom'.
599. ni...resistat: pres. subj. used instead of the imperf. to make it more vivid and indicate that the *cura* would continue, 'if my concern was not opposing'.
600. tulerint: 'would have carried them off'; on this tense see previous note. **inimicus**: with *ensis*. **hauserit**: 'would have devoured'.
601f. tibi: an example of the so-called ethic dat., 'I tell you'. **non...Paris**: two subjects, *facies Tyndaridis* and *culpatus Paris*, are said not to have destroyed Troy, 'it is not the hateful face (*facies invisa*) of the Spartan daughter of Tyndaris or (*-ve*) wicked Paris that...'. **culpatus**: in the sense of *culpandus*. **divum**: for *divorum*. What was really responsible for Troy's destruction was *inclementia divum*; insert 'but' before this new subj. Note the repeated *divum*.
603. evertit: pres. tense. **opes**: 'power'.
604f. omnem: with *nubem eripiam* line 606. **quae**: refers to *nubem*. **tuenti**: with *tibi*. **quae obducta tuenti tibi**: 'which drawn over (*obducta*) you as you gaze (*tuenti*)...'. **visus**: obj. pl. for sg. **umida...caligat**: *umida* probably nom. sg. referring to the cloud, *circum* adv. here, 'dankly spreads a mist around'.
606f. ne time, neu recusa: two neg. imperats.; in prose these would usually be *ne* + perf. subj. or *noli* + infin. **neu**: 'and don't'. **qua**: n. pl. of *quis*, with *iussa*, 'any orders'. **praeceptis**: i.e. 'her instructions'.
608. hic: adv. 'here'. **ubi**: 'where'.
610. magnoque...tridenti: with *fundamenta*, 'dislodged with his large trident'.
612. hic: adv. 'here' also. It is as though Venus is pointing out Neptune and Juno at work in two different locations in the ruined city.
613. prima: 'in the lead'. **socium**: adj. with *agmen*, 'her allied army'.
614. ferro accincta: describing Juno, 'clad in armour'.
615. respice: Venus is speaking to Aeneas, 'look behind you'.
616. nimbo...saeva: 'shining forth from a cloud and fierce with her Gorgon-shield' (Williams); *saeva* is better taken as nom. sg.
617. ipse pater: i.e. Jupiter. **animos**: 'courage'. **vires secundas**: 'renewed strength'.
618. in: 'against'.
619. eripe fugam: a vivid phrase to emphasise the need for speed.
620. nusquam abero: a double neg. to make a strong positive, i.e. 'I will be with you everywhere'. **patrio limine**: supply *in*.
621. dixerat: with this word the poet marks the end of the direct speech; lit. 'she had spoken', i.e. 'she had done speaking'.

622f. inimica Troiae: *Troiae* is dat. sg., 'hostile to Troy', describing *magna numina.* **deum:** for *deorum.*

624. omne: with *Ilium* as subject. **visum:** supply *est.*

625. ex imo: 'from its foundations'. **verti:** pres. infin. pass., supply *visa est* from previous line, 'to be overthrown'. **Neptunia:** an ironic touch; Neptune had built the walls of the city but now we find him destroying his own handiwork.

626. ac veluti cum: 'just as when'; introducing a simile, cf. line 379. The order of the words is particularly clever; first there is the tree and then it is attacked by the farmers. We have the foliage shaking (*tremefacta*) with the blows, then the groaning of the wood (*congemuit*) and finally the fall and the debris (*ruinam*).

627. ferro accisam: 'hacked with steel'. **crebris bipennis:** with *accisam*, lit. 'with frequent axes', i.e. 'with frequent axe blows'. Probably *ferro* and *bipennibus* is a hendiadys for 'steel axes'. **instant:** 'strive' with the infin. *eruere.*

628. illa: 'it' i.e. the tree.

629. comam: so-called acc. of respect with *tremefacta*, lit. 'made to tremble in its foliage'. **concusso vertice:** an abl. abs.

630. evicta: describing the tree like a human being, 'gradually overcome (*paulatim evicta*) by its wounds'. **supremum:** with *congemuit*; note how the tree again behaves like a human being.

631. traxit ruinam: see also line 465, i.e. 'came crashing down'.

632. ducente deo: abl. abs., perhaps by this phrase Virgil means that Aeneas did not know how he managed it. **inter:** with both *flammam* and *hostes.*

633. expedior: in a reflexive sense, 'I pick my way'. **dant locum:** cf. the English phrase 'give ground'.

634. perventum ad limina: supply *est* to *perventum* for the impersonal pass.; lit. 'it was reached to the threshold', i.e. 'the threshold was reached'. **patriae:** from the adj. *patrius*, 'of my father's'.

635. domos: pl. perhaps to indicate that it was a large house. **genitor:** subject of *abnegat* in line 637. **altos:** with *montes.*

636. primum: note the repetition of this word to emphasise that Aeneas was concerned for his father most of all.

637. excisa Troia: abl. abs. 'now that Troy has been laid waste'.

638. quibus...sanguis: *quibus* is dat., *aevi* is gen. of respect with *integer*, supply *est*, 'to whom there is blood untouched by time'.

639. solidae stant vires: 'strength remains sound'. **suo robore:** there is emphasis on *suo*, 'by their own vigour'. Anchises points out that being old he has to rely on other people's strength.

640. Note the repetition of *vos.* **agitate:** 'press on with'.

641. **me:** balances *vos* in the previous line. **ducere:** 'to extend', cf. line 637.

642. **satis superque:** '[it is] enough and more [than enough] that'. **una:** with *excidia*. Hercules had captured Troy previously when Laomedon had refused to pay him for ridding the country of a monster.

643. **vidimus:** 'we' for 'I'. **superavimus:** here + dat, 'I survived'.

644. **corpus:** obj. of *adfati*, 'having bid farewell to my body'. **adfati, discedite:** translate as two imperatives, 'bid farewell to...and depart'. **sic positum:** *pono* is used of laying corpses out for burial, suggesting that Anchises was lying down; the verb *adfor* is used of bidding a last farewell to the dead.

645. **manu:** not by turning his hand on himself, but like Priam deliberately attacking the enemy. **miserebitur:** i.e. an enemy will pity him in the sense of putting him out of his misery.

646. **exuvias:** i.e. Anchises' armour. **facilis...sepulcri:** supply *est*. Since the Romans placed great importance on proper burial, this is clearly a sign of utter despair.

647f. **annos demoror:** with *iam pridem* 'I have long since been delaying the years', i.e. by living too long he has held up the progress of time. **ex quo (tempore):** 'since the time that'. **divum:** for *divorum*; *divum...rex* is reminiscent of the title of Zeus in the *Iliad* and *Odyssey*.

649. Jupiter punished Anchises, a mortal, for boasting about his love for Venus. **ventis:** 'with the blasts'. **igni:** old abl. sg. of *ignis*.

650. **memorans:** 'recounting'.

651f. **contra:** adv. 'on the contrary'. **effusi lacrimis:** supply *sumus*, 'we were flooded with tears'. **coniunxque:** *-que* here 'both'; *Creusa, Ascanius, omnis domus* and presumably Aeneas make up *nos*. **ne:** ind. command following *effusi lacrimis*, '[begging] that my father (*pater*) should not'.

653. **fatoque...incumbere:** 'to add his weight to a fate that was pressing [us] hard'; *incumbere*, lit. 'to lean on'.

654. **incepto...isdem:** a mild zeugma, both *incepto* and *in sedibus* going with *haeret*, the one theoretical and the other practical; 'he remains fixed in his purpose (*incepto*) and the same abode'.

655. **feror in arma:** since Aeneas does not actually go anywhere, perhaps 'I am prompted [to go] to the battle'. Note the repetition of *r* in this line.

656. **fortuna:** i.e. a chance of the whole family getting away to safety.

657f. **mene...sperasti:** *sperasti* for *speravisti* followed by an acc. + infin. clause; 'did you expect that I could (*me posse*) depart (*efferre pedem*), father, with you left behind (*te relicto*)'.

658. **excidit:** probably perf. **patrio:** emphatic adj., 'from a father's lips'.

659. **nihil relinqui:** acc. + infin., 'that nothing be left'.

660. **hoc sedet:** lit. 'this sits', i.e. 'this is settled'. **animo:** abl. for *in (tuo) animo*.

perituraeque: this *que* 'and' begins another clause.

661. **iuvat**: supply another *te*, lit. 'it pleases you', i.e. 'you (Anchises) are pleased', followed by *addere* and two objs., *te* and *tuos*. **isti**: *iste* is used for 'that of yours'; here dat. sg. with *leto*, 'for that death [you want]'.

663. Take *qui obtruncat* at the beginning of the line.

664. **hoc erat quod**: 'was this the reason that'; Aeneas now addresses Venus, his mother.

665. **ut**: with the subj. *cernam*, 'so that I may see', explaining *hoc* in line 664. **utque**: 'and so that'.

667. **mactatos**: going with the three objs. in line 666. **alterum in alterius sanguine**: lit. 'one in another's blood', i.e. 'in one another's blood'; *alterum* stands for each one taken separately.

668. **lux**: 'dawn'

669. **sinite revisam**: *revisam* is pres. subj., supply *ut* after *sinite*, 'allow me to revisit'. Normally *sino* is followed by the infin. rather than *ut* + subj.

671. **hinc**: adv. of time here. **accingor**: in reflexive sense, 'I gird myself'. **clipeo**: dat. sg. with *insertabam sinistram*.

672. **insertabam sinistram**: 'I was inserting my left arm in...'. **aptans**: 'fitting it on'. **me ferebam**: *fero* is often used of quick movement, 'I was rushing'.

675. **periturus**: lit. 'about to die', i.e. 'to your death'. **et**: 'too'. **in omnia**: supply something like *pericula*.

676. **aliquam expertus**: 'having tried to some degree'. **sumptis**: with *in armis*, 'in the arms you have taken up'.

677. **tutare**: sg. imperat. of *tutor*.

678. **relinquor**: goes with *coniunx*, the nearest subject; from it supply *relinquitur* to *Iulus* and *pater*. **coniunx...dicta**: *tua* with *coniunx*, 'I once said to be your wife'. By *quondam* Creusa is perhaps suggesting that she will soon be a widow.

680. **dictu**: with *mirabile*, 'wonderful to relate'; *dictu* is a supine in -*u*, a verbal noun in the abl., lit. 'in telling'.

681. **inter**: with *manus* and *ora*, 'between the hands and faces'.

682. **visus**: supply *est*; subject is *apex*. **levis**: with *apex*, 'flickering'.

683. **apex**: 'tongue [of flame]'. **tactu**: with *innoxia*, 'harmless in its touch', describing *flamma*. Supply *visa est* from *visus* to *flamma*.

684. **tempora**: here 'temples of his head'. **pasci**: pres. infin. pass. of *pasco* in reflexive sense; normally used of animals browsing, here perhaps 'to play'.

685. **trepidare**: the first of three so-called historic infins. which should be translated as past verbs with *nos* as subject. They are used to indicate a rapid series of actions. **metu**: with *pavidi*.

686. **excutere**: 'shake out'. **fontibus**: 'with water'.
688. **caelo**: dat. sg., 'to the sky'. **cum voce**: i.e. 'as he spoke'.
690. **hoc tantum**: 'just this' (Williams), supply *precor*; cf. line 79.
691. Anchises is asking Jupiter to give a second omen to prove that the first was not just an insignificant accident.
692. **senior**: = *senex*. **ea**: n. pl. acc., 'those [words]'.
693. **intonuit laevum**: impers. verb, 'it thundered on the left'; *laevum* is adv. Thunder on the left was considered a good omen by the Romans. **lapsa**: perf. partic. of *labor*, here with pres. meaning.
694. **facem ducens**: 'trailing a light', i.e. a shooting star. **cucurrit**: 'sped'.
695. **illam**: obj. of *cernimus*. **super**: with *summa culmina*.
696f. **Idaea silva**: abl. sg., supply *in*. **claram**: 'shining brightly'. **limite**: the track of the star across the sky; *sulcus* is the trail that it left.
698. **late circum**: double adv. phrase, 'far and wide all around'.
699. **hic vero**: 'then indeed'. **victus**: 'convinced'. **tollit**: up to now Anchises had been lying down. **ad auras**: a poetic flourish, 'up'.
701. **nulla mora**: i.e. 'there is no delay for me'. **qua**: 'where'.
702. **di**: for *dei*. **domum**: here 'household' or 'family'.
703. **vestrum...vestro**: note the emphasis; supply *est* to the first part. **numine**: 'divine power', i.e. 'protection' (Williams).
704. **cedo**: i.e. 'I give in'. **tibi comes**: 'as a companion to you'.
705. **dixerat**: see note to line 621. **clarior**: translate as an adv., 'more distinctly'.
706. **aestus**: obj. pl. This word has meanings both of a swelling tide and a fiery heat; translate perhaps by 'billows of heat'.
707. **imponere**: sg. pass. imperat. with a reflexive meaning, 'place yourself on' + dat. **nostrae**: for *meae*, as commonly in poetry.
708. **subibo**: lit. 'I will go under', i.e. 'I will support [you]'. **umeris**: abl. pl. 'with my shoulders'. **iste**: 'that [of yours]'.
709. **quo...cumque**: this word has been split to help the metre. **res**: pl. subject. **cadent**: lit. 'will fall', i.e. 'will turn out'; this is a metaphor of the fall of dice. **periclum**: shortened form of *periculum*.
710. **ambobus**: dat. pl., supply *nobis*. **mihi**: with *comes*, see line 704.
711. **sit**: pres. subj. for a wish, 'let Iulus be'. **servet vestigia**: pres. subj. also, 'let her keep to', i.e. 'let her follow [my] footsteps'.
712. **quae dicam**: fut. tense, 'what I will say'; this is the real obj. of *advertite*. **animis**: dat. pl.; cf. the similar dat. in line 707.
713. **est...egressis**: supply *eis*, lit. 'there is for those who have gone out'.
714. **desertae**: probably 'of forlorn Ceres'; Ceres spent half the year in mourning for her daughter, Proserpina. Note the presence here of a cypress tree, the tree associated with death. See Williams' informative note on this line.

715. religione patrum: 'by the reverence of our ancestors'. **servata**: with *cupressus*.

716. ex diverso: 'from different directions'.

717. sacra: 'sacred objects'. Anchises, as head of the household, was responsible for the religious items of the family. The *sacra* would have been small vessels and utensils, the *penates* small statues.

718f. me....attrectare: acc. + infin. after *nefas*; supply *est* to *nefas*, 'it is wrong that I should touch [them]'. **vivo**: i.e. 'flowing'.

721. latos...colla: a phrase of two objs. after *insternor* which has a reflexive sense here, 'I cover my broad shoulders and bowed neck'.

722. veste: with *pelle* as a hendiadys, lit. 'with a covering and a skin', i.e. 'with the covering of a skin'. **super**: an adv. here, 'on top'.

723f. succedo: lit. 'I undergo', i.e. 'I submit to' + dat. **dextrae**: dat. sg. with *implicuit*, lit. 'he entwined himself with [my] hand' i.e. 'he clasped my hand'. **non**: with *aequis*, i.e. 'unequal'.

725. ferimur: see note to line 588, 'we rush'. **opaca locorum**: see note to line 332, i.e. 'dark places'.

726. me: obj. of *terrent* and *excitat* in line 728. **non ulla iniecta**: a phrase describing *tela*, 'no hurled weapons'.

727. tela: subject of *movebant* as is *Grai*. **ex agmine adverso**: 'in opposing rank'; *ex* is used in phrases with the sense of 'in' or 'on'.

729. suspensum: describing *me*.

731f. evasisse: this verb can take an obj. in the sense of 'escape from'; here perhaps translate as 'to have got to the end of'. **subito cum**: 'when suddenly'. **creber**: with *sonitus pedum*, lit. 'the frequent sound of feet', i.e. 'the sound of many feet'. **visus**: supply *est*.

735f. hic: adv. of time here. **nescio quod male amicum numen**: 'some unknown (*nescio quod*) unfriendly (*male amicum*) divine power'; *male* has the same force as *non*. **mihi trepido**: 'from me in my fear'. **eripuit**: followed by acc. and dat.

736. avia: n. pl. of the adj. used as a noun, 'by-ways' (Williams). **cursu**: 'at a run'.

738f. misero: supply *mihi*, after *erepta*. **fatone...erravitne...seu lassa**: three possible reasons why Creusa disappeared. The disjointed nature of this sentence reflects Aeneas' emotional turmoil over the loss of his wife. **misero...resedit**: three quests. with *incertum*, 'whether...or...or'.

740. incertum: supply *est*. **post**: an adv. here, 'afterwards'.

741. prius: take with *quam* in line 742, 'before' or 'until'. Note the repeated *re-* of the verbs emphasising the direction his eyes and mind should have taken.

742. tumulum, sedem: in poetry, the destination of movement is sometimes expressed by the acc. without a preposition.

743. omnibus una: note the significant positioning of these two words.

744. comites: this is explained by the next two nouns.

745. quem: with *hominumque deorumque*. Note the most unusual elision of the final syllable before *aut* in the next line.

747. Anchisen: Gk. acc.

748. recondo: supply *eos*.

749. cingor: in a reflexive sense, 'I gird myself'.

750. stat: lit. 'it stands', 'it is fixed', i.e. 'I am resolved to' + infins. **renovare**: lit. 'renew', i.e. 'to face again'. **casus**: acc. pl.

751. caput: i.e. 'my life'.

752. muros...limina: obj. phrase with *repeto*. **portae**: i.e. the city gate.

753f. qua: adv. 'where'. **vestigia...observata**: obj. phrase after *sequor*, '[my] footsteps traced back'.

754. lumine lustro: 'I survey with my gaze'; *lumine = oculo*.

756. domum: after *me refero*. Note the repeat of *si forte*, 'if only, if only', marking Aeneas' last pathetic hope. **tulisset**: subj. of ind. speech as Aeneas is reporting his thoughts at the time of the search.

757. inruerant...tenebant: this clinical statement marks the end of his desperate hope. **tectum omne**: 'the whole building'.

759. aestus: cf. line 706. **ad auras**: i.e. 'skywards'.

761. porticibus vacuis: an abl. phrase describing the shrine of Juno. **Iunonis asylo**: abl. of place, 'in Juno's shrine'.

763. huc: i.e. Juno's shrine. **Troia**: here sg. f. nom. of the adj., with *gaza*, 'Trojan treasure'.

764. erepta: with *Troia gaza*. **mensae**: i.e. little tables for offerings.

765. auro solidi: lit. 'solid with gold', i.e. 'of solid gold'.

766. pueri...matres: part of the booty and destined to be sold as slaves. **pueri**: 'children'.

768. ausus: perf. partic. of *audeo* with pres. meaning, 'daring'. **quin etiam**: 'in fact even'. **voces**: 'cries'.

769. Creusam: '[the name] Creusa'.

771. quaerenti, ruenti: with *mihi* in line 773, 'as I was searching and rushing'. **tectis**: abl., 'among the buildings', cf. *porticibus* line 528.

773. visa: supply *est*. **nota**: abl. sg. for comparison after *maior*, 'larger than she was known [to me]'. Apparitions of gods and the dead were usually bigger than normal human size.

774. steterunt: note that the middle syllable is scanned short.

775. adfari, demere: supply *visa est* from line 773 (Williams).

776. quid iuvat: 'what use is it [to you]?' **tantum**: adv. here, 'so much'.

777. **haec**: i.e. the capture and destruction of Troy. **divum**: for *divorum*.
778. **te asportare**: acc. + infin. after *fas*, 'that you should take'.
779. **fas**: supply *est*; on *fas* see note to line 157. **ille**: 'that [great]'.
780. **exsilia**: supply *sunt*. **vastum...arandum**: supply *est* and *tibi*, 'you must plough a vast expanse of sea'.
781. **terram**: supply *ad*. **Lydius**: with *Thybris*. To the north of the Tiber lived the Etruscans who by tradition had come to Italy from Lydia in Asia Minor.
782. **virum**: for *virorum*. **leni agmine**: 'with its gentle stream'.
783. **res laetae**: lit. 'happy circumstances', i.e. 'happiness'. **regia coniunx**: i.e. Lavinia. It is interesting that Aeneas does not keep this secret from Dido. Note the alliteration of *r* in this line.
784. **parta**: supply *est*, 'has been provided'. **pelle**: sg. imperat. 'banish'. **dilectae Creusae**: an objective gen. sg., 'tears for [your] beloved Creusa'.
786. **servitum**: supine ending in *-m* is used to express purpose after a verb of motion, 'to be a slave to'.
787. **Dardanis...nurus**: Creusa proudly describes herself, 'a descendant of Dardanus and daughter-in-law of Venus.'
788. **deum**: for *deorum*. The *magna genetrix deum* was Cybele. **his oris**: supply *in*.
789. **serva**: sg. imperat. of *servo*.
790. **dedit**: i.e. *dixit*. **lacrimantem, volentem**: supply *me* to these.
792. **conatus**: supply *sum*. **collo**: dat. sg. after *circumdare bracchia*; *circumdare* is split; see note on lines 218f.
793. **frustra**: with *comprensa*, describing *imago*, 'grasped in vain'. **manus**: acc. pl., 'my hands'.
794. **par**: + dat., 'like'. **volucri somno**: 'a fleeting dream'.
795. **consumpta nocte**: an abl. abs.
796f. **ingentem numerum adfluxisse**: an acc. + infin. after *invenio*, 'that a huge number had flocked'. **admirans**: i.e. 'to my astonishment'.
798. **collectam exsilio**: 'collected for exile'.
799. **convenere**: for *convenerunt*. **parati**: after this word you need to supply something like *proficisci* (Williams) or *sequi* (Gould & Whiteley) before the next line.
800. **velim**: subj. probably for ind. speech, this clause being what the assembled crowd thought to themselves. **pelago**: abl. sg., 'over the sea'. **deducere**: this is the technical verb to lead a group of people out to a new colony.
801. **Lucifer**: the morning star was also known significantly as Venus. Note that a new day dawns as the Trojan remnants set off to find their new city.
803. **opis**: 'of help'.
804. **sublato genitore**: an abl. abs.; *sublato* from *tollo*.

VIRGIL: THE STANDING FIGURES ARE THE MUSES OF HISTORY (LEFT) AND TRAGEDY

(From a Roman mosaic found at Sousse, Tunisia,
a town near the site of the ancient Hadrumetum.)

73

APPENDIX A

Latin Verse

In English a line of verse is produced when words are arranged in a pattern by the natural stress or *ictus* of the words used. For example:

The ploúghman hómeward plóds his wéary wáy

has a pattern of unstressed syllable followed by stressed which is one of the commonest patterns in English verse. On the other hand if we write

Hómeward plóds the plóughman his wéary wáy

we do not have a line of verse since there is no regular pattern.

In early Latin verse also the pattern was formed by the natural stress of the words used. For example:

málum dábunt Metélli Náevio póetae

is a line of verse in the early Saturnian metre, and verse with stress patterns continued to flourish in less educated circles as is indicated by the following line of a military marching song:

écce Cáesar núnc triúmphat qúi subégit Gálliás.

The Latin Hexameter

A great change occurred in Latin poetry when the Romans, influenced by Greek verse and especially Homer's *Iliad* and *Odyssey*, adopted the metre of the Greek hexameter and instead of a stress pattern based their verse on the *quantities of the syllables*. Often the quantity of a syllable coincides with the natural stress, but this is by no means always the case.

Syllables in the Latin hexameter must contain either a vowel or a diphthong and are divided into two groups: those that are considered long/heavy (marked –) and those considered short/light (marked ᴗ). In general long syllables are considered to be twice the duration of short syllables. Furthermore a syllable containing a short vowel is considered to be long/heavy if the vowel is followed by two consonants though the vowel itself remains short. (For rules on the quantity of particular vowels see below.)

The hexameter consists of six metrical units called *feet*. The first four feet are either *dactyls* (– ∪ ∪) or *spondees* (– –), the fifth foot is nearly always a *dactyl* and the sixth is either a *spondee* or a *trochee* (– ∪). So the hexameter pattern looks like this:

1	2	3	4	5	6
–∪∪	–∪∪	–∪∪	–∪∪	–∪∪	– –
– –	– –	– –	– –		–∪

and a straightforward example is:

sed si|tantus a|mor|ca|sus cog|noscere|nostros (10)

In most lines a break or *caesura* occurs after the first syllable of either the third or fourth foot; in the line quoted above the caesura falls in the third foot between *amor* and *casus*. Other breaks may be used for particular effect. This *caesura* in the middle of the line, varying as it does between two feet, helps to soften the relentless hexameter pattern and allows the poetry to flow more freely from one line to the next.

Elision is also frequent in Virgil's hexameters. This occurs when a word ending with a vowel or an 'm' is followed by a word beginning with a vowel or an 'h'. In such cases the final syllable of the first word is lost, being slurred into the first syllable of the second word. For example *Troia est* (703) and *ipsum ut* (60) become two syllables, *quaeque ipse* (5) and *comitem et* (86) become three and *uno ordine* (102) and *quamquam animus* (12) become four.

Scansion

To scan the following hexameter:

ingentes uterumque armato milite complent

1. Mark in any elision.

ingentes uterumque armato milite complent

2. Count back five syllables from the end and mark them dactyl and spondee or dactyl and trochee.

ingentes uterumque armato|milite|complent

3. Count the remaining syllables; here there are nine. This indicates that one dactyl and three spondees are required in the first four feet.

4. Mark any syllables you are sure are long.

ingentes uterumque armato|milite|complent

75

5. Complete the scansion to give one dactyl and three spondees and indicate the caesura (here in the third foot).

$$\bar{\ } \ \bar{\ } \ | \ \bar{\ } \ \smile\smile \ | \ \bar{\ } \ \| \ \bar{\ } \ | \ \bar{\ } \ \bar{\ } \ | \ \bar{\ }\smile\smile \ | \ \bar{\ } \ \ \bar{\ }$$

ingent|es uter|umq|ue ar|mato|milite|complent

The above mechanical way of scanning will always give the right answer but *it cannot be stressed too strongly* that the best way to appreciate the metre of Virgil, or of any other poet, is to read his verses aloud. Read them naturally, as if they were prose, and do not try to force them into some metrical pattern. If you pronounce words correctly, and omit or slur elided syllables, the rhythm of the verse will emerge of its own accord. There is no harm in learning the formal pattern or in scanning some lines with paper and pencil, but it is much more important *to keep on reading the verses aloud* until you can hear their swing and rhythm at the first reading.

For example you will easily hear the thud of the Cyclopes' hammers in
    illi inter sese magna vi bracchia tollunt,
the hoofs of a galloping horse in
    quadrupedante putrem sonitu quatit ungula campum,
and little Iulus trying to keep up with the big strides of his father in
    implicuit sequiturque patrem non passibus aequis.

General Notes

(a) 'h' does not count as either a vowel or a consonant. It therefore cannot help to lengthen a syllable nor does it prevent elision.

    e.g. in *meminisse horret* '– e' is elided and in *manus hic* '– us' is not lengthened.

(b) The letter 'i' as well as being a vowel is sometimes a consonant, sounding like an English 'y' as in 'yet' for example. In such cases elision is avoided.

    e.g. in *portae iuvat* there is no elision.

(c) The 'u' after 'q' is part of the consonant and not a separate vowel. Another much less common variation of this is the 'u' after the letter 'g'.

    e.g. *quorum* is two, *not* three syllables and *sanguine* is three, *not* four syllables.

Some Rules for Deciding the Quantity of a Syllable:

1. Any vowel followed by two consonants normally produces a long syllable,

    e.g. *defendit* and *quis talia.*

But if the two consonants are in the same word and the second is 'r' or 'l', the vowel, if naturally short, may remain short or become long,

         ᵕ   ᵕ   ᵕ   ᵕ ᵕ

e.g. *patris* and *lacrimantem*, *reflexi* and *crinemque flagrantem*, but if the vowel is naturally long, it remains long,
e.g. *ātra*.

2. 'x' and 'z' are double consonants.

3. All diphthongs are long,

e.g. *quae, audire* and *foedare*.

4. If two vowels come together and do not form a diphthong, the first is usually short,

e.g. *talia, Hectoreum* and *duorum*.

Exceptions are Greek words (where the Latin vowel represents a Greek diphthong or long vowel) and the 'i' of *fio*,

e.g. *Aeneas*; *fiam*.

Note however that in *fio* 'i' before 'er' is short, e.g. *fieri*.

5. Final 'i' is usually long,

e.g. *fracti, audi, forti*; but in *mihi, tibi, sibi, ubi, ibi* it is optional and in *nisi* it is short.

6. Final 'o' is usually long,

e.g. *caelo, amo* and *rogabo*, but in *ego, duo, cito* and the adverb *modo* it is short.

7. Final 'u' is always long,

e.g. *gradu*.

8. Final 'a' is short in the nominative and vocative feminine singular of nouns and adjectives, and in neuter plurals,

e.g. *insula* (nom.), *sidera*.

Elsewhere it is long,

e.g. *fama* (abl.) and *ama* (imperative).

9. Final 'e' is long in the second conjugation singular imperative active, adverbs, fifth declension ablative singular and pronouns,

e.g. *mone*; *late*; *die*; *me, te, se*.

Elsewhere it is short,

e.g. *triste*; *rege*; *domine*; *milite* and the irregular adverbs *bene, male*.

APPENDIX B

Irregularities of Scansion in *Aeneid* Book II

1. Two vowels side by side treated as one sound:

dēinde (391, 691); cūi (71, 121, 547, 677).

2. Abnormal lenghthening:

pāvor et (369); obruimūr oriturque (411); domūs et (563).

3. Older quantity retained:

stetĕrunt (774).

4. Fifth foot spondee:

constitit atque oculis Phrygia agmina|cīrcūm|spexit (68).

4. Hypermetric -*que*, elided before beginning of next line:

(745-6)...deorum(que) aut quid...

VOCABULARY

NOTE unusual meanings are followed by line reference(s)

a, ab *prep. with abl.* from
abdo -ere -didi -ditum hide;
plunge (553)
abeo -īre -ii -itum go away
abiēs abietis *f.* pine-tree, fir
abluo -ere -lui -lūtum cleanse,
purify
abnego -āre -āvi -ātum refuse
abstineo -ēre -tinui -tentum
refrain, abstain
absum -esse āfui be away from,
be absent
ac *conj.* and
accīdo -ere -cīdi -cīssum cut, hew
accingo -ere -cinxi -cinctum gird
oneself
accipio -ere -cēpi -ceptum
receive; hear (65, 308)
accommodo -āre -āvi -ātum fit,
adapt
ācer acris acre *adj.* violent, fierce
acernus -a -um *adj.* of maple
aciēs -ēi *f.* battle-line
ad *prep. with acc.* to, towards; at
addo -ere -didi -ditum add; attach
adeō *adv.* indeed
adflīgo -ere -flīxi -flictum cast down
adflo -āre -āvi -ātum breathe on,
blow on
adfluo -ere -fluxi flow to, flock to
adfor -fāri -fātus address, speak
to
adglomero -āre -āvi -ātum
assemble at
adgredior -gredi -gressus set
about, venture
adhūc *adv.* still
aditus -ūs *m.* entrance, approach

admīror -āri -mīrātus wonder at,
admire
adōro -āre -āvi -ātum revere
adsentio -īre -sēnsi -sēnsum
agree, approve
adservo -āre -āvi -ātum guard
adsum -esse adfui be present
adversus -a -um *adj.* opposing
adverto -ere -verti -versum turn to
adytum -i *n.* shrine
aedēs -is *f.* sanctuary, dwelling
aedifico -āre -āvi -ātum build
aeger -gra -grum *adj.* sick, weary
aēnus -a -um *adj.* of bronze
aequaevus -a -um *adj.* of like age
aequo -āre -āvi -ātum equal,
match
aequor -oris *n.* sea, surface (780)
aequus -a -um *adj.* fair, just; equal
aerātus -a -um *adj.* covered with
bronze
aes aeris *n.* bronze
aestus -ūs *m.* heat
aetās -tātis *f.* age
aeternus -a -um *adj.* eternal
aethēr -eris *m.* air, sky
aevum -i *n.* age
ager agri *m.* field
agger -eris *m.* mound; barrier
agitātor -ōris *m.* driver
agito -āre -āvi -ātum pursue, hunt
agmen -inis *n.* rank; multitude;
line of march; course (782)
agnosco -ere -gnōvi -gnitum
recognise
ago -ere ēgi actum drive;
(*imperat.*) age come on!
agricola -ae *m.* farmer

79

aio *defect. verb* say
aliqui aliqua aliquod *indef. adj.*
 some, any
aliquis aliquid *indef. pron.*
 someone something
aliter *adv.* otherwise
alius alia aliud *adj.* other
almus -a -um *adj.* kind, gentle
altāria ium *n.pl.* altar
alter -era -erum *adj.* the one/the
 other (of two)
altus -a -um *adj.* high; deep
alvus -i *f.* belly
ambiguus -a -um *adj.* uncertain
ambo -ae -o *pl. adj.* both
āmens -entis *adj.* out of one's mind
amīcus -a -um *adj.* friendly
amīcus -i *m.* friend
āmitto -ere -mīsi -missum lose
amnis -is *m.* river
amor -ōris *m.* love
amplector -i amplexus embrace
amplus -a -um *adj.* large, extensive
an *conj.* or
anguis -is *c.* snake
angustus -a -um *adj.* narrow
anima -ae *f.* life
animus -i *m.* mind; spirit; courage
annus -i *m.* year
ante *adv.* before, previously
ante *prep. with acc.* before
antīquus -a -um *adj.* ancient, old,
 former
aperio -īre -ui -ertum open
apex -icis *m.* point, top
appāreo -ere -ui -itum appear
apto -āre -āvi -ātum fit
apud *prep with acc.* among, with
āra -ae *f.* altar
arbor -oris *f.* tree
arceo -ēre -ui restrain, confine
ardeo -ēre arsi arsum be on fire,
 burn; gleam (734); be eager

arduus -a -um *adj.* towering
ariēs -etis *m.* ram; battering ram
arma -ōrum *n.pl.* arms
armātus -a -um *adj.* armed
armentum -i *n.* herd, flock
armipotēns -entis *adj.* powerful
 in arms
armo -āre -āvi -ātum arm
aro -āre -āvi -ātum plough
arrigo -ere arrēxi arrectum lift
 up, raise
ars artis *f.* skill; cunning
artifex -icis *m.* schemer
artus -a -um *adj.* tight
artus -ūs *m. usually pl.* limb
arvum -i *n.* land, field
arx arcis *f.* citadel, place of refuge
 (322)
ascendo -ere -scendi -scensum go up
ascensus -ūs *m.* climbing
asper -era -erum *adj.* bitter,
 harsh; prickly (379)
aspicio -ere -spēxi -spectum look
 at, see
aspiro -āre -āvi -ātum breathe on,
 favour
asporto -āre -āvi -ātum carry away
ast *conj.* but, yet
asto -āre astiti stand
astrum -i *n.* star
asȳlum -i *n.* sanctuary
at *conj.* but
āter ātra ātrum *adj.* black
atque *conj.* and
atrium -i *n.* hall
attollo -ere raise, erect
attrecto -āre -āvi -ātum touch,
 handle
auctor -ōris *c.* originator
audeo -ēre ausus sum dare
audio -īre -īvi -ītum hear, listen
 to; heed
augurium -i *n.* augury, omen

aura -ae *f.* breeze

aurātus -a -um *adj.* covered with
gold

aureus -a -um *adj.* golden

auris -is *f.* ear

aurum -i *n.* gold

ausum -i *n.* daring deed

aut *conj.* or

aut...aut either...or

autem *conj.* but

auxilium -i *n.* help

āveho -ere -vēxi -vectum carry away

āvello -ere -vulsi -vulsum tear away

āverto -ere -verti -versum turn away

āvius -a -um *adj.* out of the way

avus -i *m.* grandfather

axis -is *m.* axis of the earth

barba -ae *f.* beard

barbaricus -a -um *adj.* foreign

bellum -i *n.* war

bīgae -ārum *f. pl.* two-horse chariot

bipatens -entis *adj.* double

bipennis -is *f.* two-edged axe

bīs *adv.* twice

bōs bovis *c.* ox

bracchium -i *n.* arm

breviter *adv.* briefly

brūma -ae *f.* winter

cado -ere cecidi cāsum fall

caecus -a -um *adj.* secret; dark;
blinded (244)

caedēs -is *f.* slaughter

caedo -ere cecīdi caesum cut down,
slay

caelicola -ae *c.* god

caelum -i *n.* sky, heaven

caerulus -a -um *adj.* dark blue,
dark green

cālīgo -āre be dark, gloomy

campus -i *m.* plain

cano -ere cecini cantum sing; foretell

capio -ere cēpi captum capture,
take, seize

captīvus -a -um *adj.* captive

capulus -i *m.* hilt

caput -itis *n.* head

cardo -inis *m.* hinge

careo -ēre -ui -itum be without

carīna -ae *f.* keel, ship

cārus -a -um *adj.* dear

cassus -a -um *adj. with abl.*
deprived of

castra -ōrum *n.pl.* camp

cāsus -ūs *m.* chance, misfortune

caterva -ae *f.* crowd

catulus -i *c.* cub, whelp

causa -ae *f.* cause

caverna -ae *f.* cavity, cavern

cavo -āre -āvi -ātum carve out

cavus -a -um *adj.* hollow,
enfolding (360)

cēdo -ere cessi cessum give way,
yield; go away

celsus -a -um *adj.* lofty

centum *indecl. adj.* a hundred

cerno -ere crēvi crētum see

certātim *adv.* vying with one
another, eagerly

certo -āre -āvi -ātum contend,
fight, vie (64)

certus -a -um *adj.* fixed, sure,
definite

cervix -icis *f.* neck

cesso -āre -āvi -ātum cease

cēterus -a -um *adj.* the other,
remaining

ceu *conj.* just as, like

cieo -ēre cīvi cītum rouse, stir up

cingo -ere cinxi cinctum gird on

cinis -eris *m.* ashes

circum *adv.* around, round about

circum *prep. with acc.* around

circumdo -āre -dedi -datum put
around

circumfundo -ere -fūdi -fūsum
pour round

circumspicio -ere -spēxi -spectum
look round at
circumsto -āre-steti stand around,
encompass
circumvolo -āre -āvi -ātum fly
around
civis civis *c.* citizen
clādēs -is *f.* disaster, massacre
clāmor -ōris *m.* shout, shouting
clangor -ōris *m.* blaring
clāresco -ere clārui become
distinct
clārus -a -um *adj.* bright, clear
classis -is *f.* fleet
claustrum -i *n.* bar, bolt
clipeus -i *m.* shield
coeptus -a -um *perf. partic.* begun
cognosco -ere cognōvi cognitum
learn,
cōgo -ere coēgi coactum force,
compel
colligo -ere -lēgi -lectum collect,
gather together
collum -i *n.* neck
coluber -bri *m.* snake
columba -ae *f.* dove
coma -ae *f.* hair; foliage (629)
comans -antis *adj.* crested, plumed
comes -itis *c.* companion
comitor -āri comitātus accompany
commendo -āre -āvi -ātum entrust
commūnis -e *adj.* common
compāgēs -is *f.* fastening, joint
compello -āre -āvi -ātum
address
complector -i -plexus embrace
compleo -ēre -plēvi -plētum fill
compositō *adv.* by agreement
comprendo -ere -endi -ensum seize
comprimo -ere -pressi -pressum
restrain, check
concēdo -ere -cessi -cessum
depart, retire

concido -ere -cidi fall, collapse
concilium -i *n.* council
conclāmo -āre -āvi -ātum shout
together
concrētus -a -um *adj.* matted
together
concurro -ere -curri -cursum run
together
concutio -ere -cussi -cussum shake
violently
condensus -a -um *adj.* huddled
together
condo -ere -didi -ditum bury; hide
confertus -a -um *adj.* close packed
configo -ere -fixi -fixum pierce
confiteor -ēri -fessus reveal self
(591)
confligo -ere -flixi -flictum
contend, fight
confundo -ere -fūdi -fūsum throw
into confusion
congemo -ere -ui -itum groan
loudly
congero -ere -gessi -gestum
heap up
congredior -i -gressus engage (in
battle)
cōnicio -ere -iēci -iectum throw,
hurl
coniugium -i *n.* husband
coniunx -iugis *c.* husband, wife
cōnor -āri conātus try
consanguinitās -tātis *f.* blood
relationship
conscius -a -um *adj.* knowing,
aware; confederate (267)
consequor -i -secūtus accompany
consero -ere -serui -sertum *with*
proelium fight at close quarters
consīdo -ere -sēdi -sessum settle,
sink down
consilium -i *n.* advice, plan
consisto -ere -stiti -stitum stand still

conspectus -ūs *m.* sight, view

consūmo -ere -sumpsi -sumptum
take up totally

contexo -ere -texui -textum
interweave, construct

conticesco -ere -ui become silent

contineo -ēre -tinui -tentum hold
back, restrain

contingo -ere -tigi -tactum touch,
take hold of

contorqueo -ēre -torsi -tortum
hurl

contrā *adv.* in reply; in return;
on the other hand (651)

contrārius -a -um *adj.* opposing

convello -ere -velli -vulsum tear up

convenio -īre -vēni -ventum come
together, meet

converto -ere -verti -versum turn,
change

convolvo -ere -volvi -volūtum roll
together

cōpia -ae *f.* force, number

cōram *prep. with abl.* in presence of

corpus -oris *n.* body

corripio -ere -ripui -reptum seize

coruscus -a -um *adj.* flashing

costa -ae *f.* rib

crātēr -ēris *m.* bowl

crēber -bra -brum *adj.* frequent,
repeated

crēdo -ere crēdidi crēditum
believe, trust (*with dat.*)

cresco -ere crēvi crētum grow,
spring

crīmen -inis *n.* charge

crīnis -is *m.* hair

crūdēlis -e *adj.* cruel

cruentus -a -um *adj.* bloodstained

culmen -inis *n.* peak, summit;
roof-top

culpa -ae *f.* fault, blame

culpo -āre -āvi -ātum blame

cum *conj.* when, since

cum *prep with abl.* with

cumulus -i *m.* heap

cunctus -a -um *adj.* all

cupīdo -inis *f.* desire

cupio -ere -īvi *or* -ii -ītum desire

cupressus -i *f.* cypress-tree

cūr *conj.* why?

cūra -ae *f.* care, concern

cūro -āre -āvi -ātum care for,
attend to

curro -ere cucurri cursum run

cursus -ūs *m.* running

curvus -a -um *adj.* curved

cuspis -idis f. point, *hence* spear

custōs -ōdis *m.* guard

dē *prep. with abl.* down from, from

dea -ae *f.* goddess

dēbeo -ēre -ui -itum owe

decem *indecl.* ten

decōrus -a -um *adj.* handsome,
elegant

dēcurro -ere -curri -cursum
run down

decus -oris *n.* honour

dēdūco -ere -dūxi -ductum lead away

dēfendo -ere -fendi -fensum defend

dēfensor -ōris *m.* protector,
defender

dēfessus -a -um *adj.* tired

dēficio -ere -fēci -fectum fail, be
missing

dēgener -eris *adj.* degenerate

deinde *adv.* then, next

dēlābor -i -lapsus fall into

dēligo -ere dēlēgi delectum choose

dēlitesco -ere -litui hide oneself

dēlūbrum -i *n.* shrine, temple

dēmens -entis *adj.* out of one's mind

dēmitto -ere -mīsi -missum send
down, lower (262)

dēmo -ere dempsi demptum
remove

dēmoror -āri -morātus detain,
delay
dēmum *adv.* at length
dēnique *adv.* at length, finally
dēnsus -a -um closely-packed
dēpascor -i -pastus feed on,
devour
dēpōno -ere -posui -positum put
down, lay aside
dēscendo -ere -di -sum go down,
descend
dēsero -ere -ui -tum desert
dēsertus -a -um *adj.* deserted
destino -āre -āvi -ātum appoint,
mark out
dēsuētus -a -um *adj.* disused, laid
aside
dēsum -esse -fui be missing
dēsuper *adv.* down from above
dētineo -ēre -tinui -tentum keep
back
deus -i *m.* god
dēvolvo -ere -volvi -volūtum roll
down
dextra -ae *f.* right hand
dīco -ere dixi dictum speak, say
dictum -i *n.* word
diēs -ēi *m. or f.* day
diffugio -ere -fūgi flee in different
directions
dīgero -ere -gessi -gestum explain
dīgnus -a -um *adj.* worthy, deserved
dīgredior -i -gressus go away,
depart
dīlectus -a -um *adj.* beloved
dīripio -ere -ripui -reptum plunder
dīrus -a -um *adj.* dreadful, terrible
discēdo -ere -cessi -cessum depart
disco -ere didici learn
discors -ordis *adj.* disagreeing,
at variance
dīsicio -ere -iēci -iectum scatter;
dash in pieces

diū *adv.* for a long time
dīva -ae *f.* goddess
dīvello -ere -vulsi *or* -velli -vulsum
tear apart
dīversus -a -um *adj.* in different
directions
dīves divitis *adj.* rich
dīvido -ere -vīsi -vīsum break through
dīvīnus -a -um divine
dīvus -i *m.* god
do dare dedi datum give, grant
dolor -ōris *m.* grief
dolus -i *m.* deceit, trickery
dominor -āri -ātus be master,
be ruler
domo -āre domui domitum subdue
domus -ūs *or* -i *f.* house, home
dōnec *conj.* until
dōnum -i *n.* gift
draco -ōnis *m.* serpent
dubius -a -um *adj.* doubtful,
uncertain
dūco -ere duxi ductum lead, bring,
take, draw; lengthen (641)
ductor -ōris *m.* leader
dūdum *adv.* lately
dulcis -e *adj.* sweet
dum *conj.* while, until
duo -ae -o two
dūrus -a -um *adj.* harsh; tough,
stubborn (479)
dux ducis *m.* leader
ē *prep. with abl.* from
ecce *demons. adv.* behold!
edax -ācis *adj.* devouring,
consuming
ēdissero -ere -disserui explain
ēdūco -ere -duxi -ductum raise,
build up
effero -ferre extuli ēlātum bring
out, carry away; raise
effigiēs -ēi *f.* image, statue
effor -āri effātus speak out, utter

84

effugio -ere -fūgi flee away, escape
effugium -i *n.* escape
effulgeo -ēre -fulsi shine forth
effundo -ere -fūdi -fūsum pour forth
egeo -ēre -ui need (*with abl.*)
ego *pron.* I
ēgredior -i egressus go out
ēlābor -i -lapsus escape
ēmico -āre -micui -micātum spring forth
ēmoveo -ere -mōvi -mōtum move out
enim *conj.* for
ensis -is *m.* sword
eo īre īvi *or* **ii itum** go
equidem *adv.* for my part
equus -i *m.* horse
ergō *adv.* therefore
ēripio -ere -ripui -retum snatch away
erro -āre -āvi -ātum wander, roam
error -ōris *m.* deception
ērubesco -ere -ui feel shame; respect
ēruo -ere ērui ērutum overthrow
et *conj.* and
etiam *adv.* also, even
etsī *conj.* even if, although
ēvādo -ere -vāsi -vāsum go out, escape, emerge (531)
ēvenio -īre -vēni -ventum turn out
ēverto -ere -verti -versum overthrow
ēvinco -ere -vīci -victum overcome completely
ex *prep. with abl.* from
exardesco -ere -arsi -arsum blaze out
excēdo -ere -cessi -cessum go out, depart
excidium -i *n.* destruction, overthrow
excido -ere -cīdi -cīsum cut out; destroy (637)

excido -ere -cidi fall from
excindo -ere -cidi -scissum destroy, raze
excito -āre -āvi -ātum rouse
exclāmo -āre -āvi -ātum shout out, exclaim
excutio -ere -cussi -cussum rouse, waken, shake off
exeo -īre -ii -itum go out
exercitus -ūs *m.* army
exhālo -āre -āvi -ātum breathe out
exigo -ere -ēgi -actum drive out
exitiālis -e destructive, fatal
exitium -i *n.* destruction
exitus -ūs *m.* departure; death
exoptātus -a -um *adj.* longed for
exorior -īri -ortus rise
expedio -īre -ii *or* **īvi -ītum** extricate
expendo -ere -pendi -pensum pay for
experior -īri expertus try, put to the test
expleo -ēre -ēvi -ētum fill up; satisfy
explico -āre -āvi *or* **-ui -ātum** unfold, set out
exprōmo -ere -prompsi -promptum utter
exsanguis -e *adj.* bloodless, pale
exsilium -i *n.* exile
exspecto -āre -āvi -ātum wait for; long for (283)
exstinguo -ere -stinxi -stinctum put an end to
exsulto -āre -āvi -ātum leap up, exult
exsupero -āre -āvi -ātum tower above
extemplō *adv.* at once
extrā *prep. with acc.* outside
extrēmus -a -um *adj.* farthest, extreme, last

exuo -ere -ui -utum strip
exuviae -ārum *f. pl.* spoils; skin
(473)
fabricātor -ōris *m.* builder,
contriver
fabrico -āre -āvi -ātum construct,
build
faciēs -ēi *f.* appearance, face
facilis -e *adj.* easy
facio -ere fēci factum make, do
factum -i *n.* deed
fallo -ere fefelli falsum deceive,
disappoint
falsus -a -um *adj.* false
fāma -ae *f.* rumour, report
famulus -i *m.* servant, attendant
fās *n. indecl. noun* right thing
fastīgium -i *n.* gable
fātālis -e *adj.* belonging to fate,
fateful
fateor -ēri fassus confess
fātum -i *n.* fate, destiny
fauces -ium *f.pl.* jaws, throat
fax facis *f.* torch; fire-ball
fēmineus -a -um *adj.* of a woman,
female
fenestra -ae *f.* window
ferio -īre strike
fero ferre tuli lātum bear, carry,
bring
ferrum -i *n.* iron, sword
ferunt *from* **fero** they say (that)
ferus -a -um *adj.* fierce, cruel
ferus -i *m.* beast
fessus -a -um *adj.* tired
festīno -āre -āvi -ātum hurry
festus -a -um *adj.* festive
fētus -a -um *adj.*pregnant
fictus -a -um *adj.* false (107)
fidēs -ēi *f.* faith, reliance, proof (309)
fīdo -ere fīsus sum put confidence
in (*with dat.*)
fīdūcia -ae *f.* reliance, confidence

fīdus -a -um *adj.* trustworthy,
trusty
fīgo -ere fīxi fīxum fix, fasten
fingo -ere finxi fictum form, make
fīnis -is *f.* end
fīo fieri factus sum become,
happen
firmo -āre -āvi -ātum confirm, ratify
firmus -a -um *adj.* strong
flāgito -āre -āvi -ātum demand
flagro -āre -āvi -ātum blaze, burn
flamma -ae *f.* flame
flecto -ere flexi flectum bend,
sway; influence
fleo -ēre flēvi flētum weep
flētus -ūs *m.* weeping, wailing
fluctus -ūs *m.* wave
flūmen -inis *n.* river
fluo -ere fluxi flow
foedo -āre -āvi -ātum defile,
pollute
fons fontis *m.* spring, fountain
(for) fāri fātus speak, say
foris -is *f.* door
formīdo -inis *f.* fear, dread
fors *abl.* **forte** *f.* chance
fors *adv.* perhaps
forsitan *adv.* perhaps
forte *adv.* by chance
fortis -e *adj.* brave
fortūna -ae *f.* fortune
fragor -ōris *m.* crash
frango -ere frēgi fractum break
fremitus -ūs *m.* roaring
fretum -i *n.* strait
frīgidus -a -um *adj.* cold
frons frondis *f.* leafy bough
frustrā *adv.* in vain
frux frūgis *f. usually pl.* produce
of the earth
fuga -ae *f.* flight, way of escape,
escape
fugio -ere fūgi flee

Vocabulary

fulgeo -ēre -si glitter, shine
fulmen -inis *n.* thunderbolt,
  lightning
fulvus -a -um *adj.* tawny
fūmo -āre -āvi -ātum smoke
fūmus -i *m.* smoke
fundāmentum -i *n.* foundation
fundo -ere fūdi fūsum pour, shed;
  rout (421)
fundus -i *m.* bottom
fūnis -is *m.* rope
fūnus -eris *n.* funeral, death
furio -āre -āvi -ātum madden,
  enrage
furo -ere furui rage, rave
furor -ōris *m.* frenzy, rage
furtim *adv.* stealthily
futūrus -a -um *fut. partic. of* sum
galea -ae *f.* helmet
gaudeo -ēre gāvīsus sum rejoice
gāza -ae *f.* treasure
gelidus -a -um *adj.* cold
geminus -a -um *adj.* twin
gemitus -ūs *m.* groan, groaning
gener -eri *m.* son-in-law
genetrix -īcis *f.* mother
genitor -ōris *m.* father
gens gentis *f.* nation, family
genus -eris *n.* kind, sort
gero -ere gessi gestum bear, carry,
  wear
glomero -āre -āvi -ātum assemble
glōria -ae *f.* glory
gradus -ūs *m.* step, rung
grāmen -inis *n.* grass
grātes (*nom. and acc. pl. only*) *f.*
  thanks
grātus -a -um *adj.* welcome
gravis -is *adj.* heavy, weighed down
graviter *adv.* heavily, deeply
gravo -āre -āvi -ātum weigh
  down, oppress
gressus -ūs *m.* step

gurges -itis *m.* whirlpool, swirling
  water
habeo -ēre -ui -itum have, hold
haereo -ēre haesi haesum stick,
  cling to
hasta -ae *f.* spear
haud *adv.* not
haurio -īre hausi haustum drain;
  devour
hebeto -āre -āvi -ātum make dull
  (605)
heu *interjection* alas!
hīc *adv.* here
hīc haec hōc *demons. pron.* this
hiems hiemis *f.* storm, winter
hinc *adv.* from here; from this
hodiē *adv.* today
homō -inis *c.* a person
horrendus -a -um *adj.* dreadful
horreo -ēre -ui shudder
horresco -ere begin to shudder
horror -ōris *m.* dread, horror
hortor -āri -ātus urge, encourage
hostia -ae *f.* sacrificial victim
hostis hostis *c.* enemy
hūc *adv.* to here
humus -i *f.* ground; *locat.* **humi**
  on the ground
iaceo -ēre iacui lie down
iacto -āre -āvi -ātum throw; utter
  (588, 768)
iactūra -ae *f.* loss
iaculor -āri iaculātus hurl
iam *adv.* now, by now; already
iamdūdum *adv.* long overdue,
  forthwith
iānua -ae *f.* door
ibi *adv.* there
ictus -ūs *m.* stroke, blow
īdem eadem idem *adj.* same
ignārus -a -um *adj.* ignorant, un-
  aware
ignis -is *m.* fire

ignōtus -a -um *adj.* not known
īlicet *adv.* immediately
ille illa illud *demons. pron.* that;
he she it
illīc *adv.* there
imāgo -inis *f.* form, appearance
imbellis -e *adj.* not fit for war,
feeble
immānis -e *adj.* enormous, huge
immemoris -e *adj.* regardless,
unmindful
immēnsus -a -um *adj.* immense,
huge
immisceo -ēre -miscui -mixtum
mingle with
immitto -ere -mīsi -missum send
in
impello -ere -puli -pulsum drive
on, push
imperium -i *n.* rule; empire
impetus -ūs *m.* attack, violence
impius -a -um *adj.* impious
impleo -ēre -plēvi -plētum fill
implico -āre -ui entwine, enfold
impōno -ere -posui -positum
place on
improbus -a -um *adj.* wicked,
unjust
imprōvidus -a -um *adj.*
unexpecting
imprōvīsus -a -um *adj.* unfore-
seen, unexpected
īmus -a -um *adj.* lowest, deepest
in *prep. with abl.* in, on, among
in *prep. with acc.* into, against
incendium -i *n.* conflagration,
fire
incendo -ere -cendi -censum burn
inceptum -i *n.* beginning, purpose
incertus -a -um *adj.* uncertain,
unsteady
incido -ere -cidi -cāsum fall upon
incipio -ere incēpi inceptum begin

inclēmentia -ae *f.* unmercifulness
inclūdo -ere -clūsi -clūsum shut in
inclutus -a -um *adj.* celebrated,
renowned
incolumis -is *adj.* unimpaired,
unharmed
incomitātus -a -um *adj.*
unaccompanied
incumbo -ere -cubui -cubitum
press upon (*with dat.*)
incurro -ere -curri -cursum run
against
incūso -āre -āvi -ātum accuse
inde *adv.* then, from there
indicium -i *n.* charge
indīgnor -āri -dignātus
am indignant at
indīgnus -a um *adj.* undeserved
indomitus -a -um *adj.*
unrestrained
indulgeo -ēre -dulsi -dultum
indulge in (*with dat.*)
induo -ere indui indutum put on,
clothe
inēluctābilis -e *adj.* inevitable
inermis -e *adj.* unarmed
iners -ertis *adj.* motionless
infandus -a -um *adj.* unspeakable
infēlix -īcis *adj.* unfortunate,
calamitous
infensus -a -um *adj.* hostile
infestus -a -um *adj.* hostile,
threatening
infula -ae *f.* headband
ingemino -āre -āvi -ātum repeat
ingens -entis *adj.* huge
ingrātus -a -um *adj.* unpleasant
ingruo -ere ingrui rush forward
inicio -ere -iēci -iectum throw into,
throw at
inimīcus -a -um *adj.* hostile
inīquus -a -um *adj.* unfair, hostile
inlābor -i -lapsus glide into

inlūdo -ere -lūsi -lūsum mock

innoxius -a -um *adj.* harmless

innuptus -a -um *adj.* unmarried

inquam, *3rd person* inquit say

inritus -a -um *adj.* useless, ineffectual

inruo -ere -rui rush at, rush into

insānia -ae *f.* madness

insānus -a -um *adj.* mad

inscius -a -um *adj.* not knowing

insequor -i -secūtus pursue

inserto -āre -āvi -ātum insert

insideo -ēre -sēdi -sessum sit oneself on

insidiae -ārum *f.pl.* ambush; stratagem

insigne -is *n.* ornament, badge

insinuo -āre -āvi -ātum penetrate

insono -āre -ui sound, resound

insons -sontis *adj.* guiltless, innocent

inspicio -ere -spēxi -spectum look into, inspect

instar *indecl. n.* likeness

instauro -āre -āvi -ātum renew, restore

insterno -ere -strāvi -strātum spread over

insto -āre -stiti -stātum press on, strive (627)

instruo -ere -struxi -structum draw up, equip

insula -ae *f.* island

insulto -āre -āvi -ātum exult

insuper *adv.* over and above, besides

integer -gra -grum *adj.* untouched by (*with gen*)

intemerātus -a -um *adj.* unviolated, undefiled

intendo -ere -tendi -tensum *or* -tentum stretch

intentus -a -um *adj.* eager, intent

inter *prep. with acc.* among, between

interclūdo -ere -clūsi -clūsum shut in, hinder

intereā *adv.* meanwhile

interior -ius *adj.* inner

intexo -ere intexui intextum weave, plait

intono -āre -tonui thunder

intorqueo -ēre -torsi -tortum hurl at

intrā *prep. with acc.* inside

intus *adv.* inside

inultus -a -um *adj* unavenged

inūtilis -e *adj.* useless

invādo -ere -vāsi -vāsum rush into

invenio -ire -veni -ventum find

inventor -ōris *m.* deviser

invidia -ae *f.* envy, jealousy

invīsus -a -um *adj.* hateful

invītus -a -um *adj.* unwilling, reluctant

involvo -ere -volvi -volūtum wrap up, envelop

ipse ipsa ipsum himself, herself, itself; self

īra -ae *f.* anger

is ea id *demons. pron.* that

iste ista istud *demons. pron.* that

ita *adv.* thus, in this way

iter -ineris *n.* route, road

iterum *adv.* again

iuba -ae *f.* crest

iubeo -ēre iussi iussum order

iugum -i *n.* mountain ridge

iunctūra -ae *f.* joint

iungo -ere iunxi iunctum join

ius iūris *n.* oath, *pl.* rights (541)

iussū *abl. sing.* by the order of

iussum -i *n.* order

iustus -a -um *adj.* just

iuvat *impers. verb* it pleases

iuvenālis -e *adj.* of one's youth
iuvenis -is *m.* young man
iuventa -ae *f.* youth
iuventūs -ūtis *f.* youth
iuvo -āre iūvi iūtum please
iuxtā *adv.* nearby
lābēs -is *f.* strike, blow
labo -āre -āvi -ātum totter
labor -ōris *m.* labour; struggle; hardship
lābor lābi lapsus glide past, slip by, slide; fall
lacrima -ae *f.* tear
lacrimo -āre -āvi -ātum shed tears
lacus -ūs *m.* lake, pool
laedo -ere laesi laesum injure, damage, offend
laetus -a -um *adj.* happy, luxuriant (306)
laeva -ae *f.* left hand
laevus -a -um *adj.* left, unfavourable (54)
lambo - ere lambi lick
lāmentābilis -e *adj.* pitiable
lapso -āre slip
lapsus -ūs *m.* gliding, slithering
largus -a -um *adj.* plentiful, copious
lassus -a -um *adj.* weary
lātē *adv.* far and wide
latebra -ae *f.* hiding-place
lateo -ēre -ui lie hidden
lātus -a um *adj.* wide, broad
latus -eris *n.* side, flank
laudo -āre -āvi -ātum praise
laurus -i *and* -ūs *f.* laurel-tree
laus laudis *f.* praise; renown
laxo -āre -āvi -ātum loosen
lego -ere lēgi lectum choose (762); skim over (208)
lēnis -e *adj.* gentle, smooth
leo leōnis *m.* lion

lētum -i *n.* death
levis -e *adj.* light
levo -āre -āvi -ātum raise, relieve
lex lēgis *f.* law
lignum -i *n.* wood
ligo -āre -āvi -ātum tie, bind
līmen -inis *n.* threshold
līmes -itis *m.* track, path
līmōsus -a -um *adj.* muddy
lingua -ae *f.* tongue
linquo -ere līqui leave
lito -āre -āvi -ātum obtain favourable omen, appease
lītus -oris *n.* shore
loco -āre -āvi -ātum place
locus -i *m.* (*pl.* loca) place, room
longaevus -a -um *adj.* aged
longē *adv.* at a distance
longus -a -um *adj.* long
loquor -i locūtus speak
lōrum -i *n.* thong
lūbricus -a -um *adj.* slippery
luctus -ūs *m.* grief
lūgeo -ēre lūxi luctum mourn, lament
lūmen -inis *n.* light; eye (173, 405, 754)
lūna -ae *f.* moon
lupus -i *m.* wolf
lustro -āre -āvi -ātum roam (528); survey (564, 754)
lux lūcis *f.* light
māchina -ae *f.* contrivance
macto -āre -āvi -ātum offer a sacrifice; slaughter
maestus -a -um *adj.* sad, sorrowful
magis *adv.* more
magnus -a -um *adj.* great, large
māior -ius *adj.* greater
male *adv.* badly
malum -i *n.* evil, misfortune
malus -a -um *adj.* bad
maneo -ēre mansi mansum

remain; await; abide by, keep
(160)

manica -ae *f.* fetter

manifestus -a -um *adj.* evident,
apparent

manus -ūs *f.* hand; band (29, 315)

mare -is *n.* sea

māter mātris *f.* mother

maximus -a -um *adj.* greatest,
mighty (339)

medius -a -um *adj.* middle (of)

melior -ius *adj.* better

memento *imperat. of* memini

memini (*infin.* **meminisse**)
remember

memorābilis -e *adj.* memorable

memoro -āre -āvi -ātum tell,
relate

mendax -ācis *adj.* lying

mens mentis *f.* mind

mensa -ae *f.* table

mentior -īri mentītus lie, deceive

mercor -āri -ātus buy, purchase

mereo -ēre -ui -itum deserve

mereor -ēri meritus deserve

metus -ūs *m.* fear

meus -a -um *adj.* my, mine

mico -āre -ui gleam; flicker

mīles -itis *m.* soldier

mīlia -ium *n.pl.* thousands

mille *indecl.* one thousand

minister -tri *m.* assistant,
accomplice, attendant

minor -āri minātus threaten

mīrābilis -e *adj.* wonderful

mīror -āri -ātus wonder at

misceo -ēre miscui mixtum mix
up, confuse

miser -era -erum *adj.* wretched,
unhappy

miserābilis -e *adj.* wretched,
miserable

misereor -ēri miseritus pity

miseresco -ere begin to pity

mitto -ere mīsi missum send

modo *adv.* only

moenia -orum *n.pl.* walls,
fortifications

mōlēs -is *f.* mass, bank of river
(497)

mōlior -īri molītus attempt

mollis -e *adj.* soft

moneo -ēre monui monitum
advise; warn

mons montis *m.* mountain

monstro -āre -āvi -ātum show,
point out

monstrum -i *n.* omen, monstrosity

montānus -a -um *adj.* of a mountain

mora -ae *f.* delay

morior -i mortuus die

moror -āri -ātus delay, detain

mors mortis *f.* death

morsus -ūs *m.* bite

mortālis -e *adj.* mortal

mortālis -is *c.* human being

moveo -ēre mōvi mōtum move,
provoke (96)

mucro -ōnis *m.* point, sword

mūgītus -ūs *m.* bellow, bellowing

multus -a -um *adj.* much; *pl.* many

mūrus -i *m.* wall

mūto -āre -āvi -ātum change

nam, namque *conj.* for

narro -āre -āvi -ātum tell, relate

nascor -i nātus be born

nāta -ae *f.* daughter

nātus -i *m.* son

nāvis -is *f.* ship

-ne *interrog. particle*

nē *conj. with subj.* lest, so that...not

nē *part. of neg. command* do not...

nebula -ae *f.* cloud

nec, neque *conj.* and not, neither,
nor

nefandus -a -um *adj.* impious

nefās *n. indecl.* impiety, wickedness
nego -āre -āvi -ātum deny
nepōs -ōtis *m.* grandson; descendant
neque, nec *conj.* and not, neither, nor
nēquīquam *adv.* in vain
nescio -īre -īvi -ītum not know
neu *conj.* and lest, and that ...not; and do not (607)
nex necis *f.* death
nī *conj.* unless
nihil *n. indecl.* nothing
nimbus -i *m.* cloud
nitidus -a -um *adj.* shining, bright
nītor -i nixus *or* **nīsus** bear down upon; climb (443)
nōdus -i *m.* knot
nōmen -inis *n.* name, reputation (583)
nōn *adv.* not
nōs *pron.* we
noster nostra nostrum *adj.* our
nōtus -a -um *adj.* known
novus -a -um *adj.* new
nox noctis *f.* night
nūdus -a -um *adj.* bare, uncovered
nullus -a -um *adj.* no
nūmen -inis *n.* divine power, divine purpose, divine favour (178, 233)
numerus -i *m.* number
numquam *adv* never
nunc *adv.* now
nuntius -i *m.* messenger
nūrus -ūs *f.* daughter-in-law
nusquam *adv.* nowhere
nūto -āre -āvi -ātum nod, sway
ō *with voc. when addressing people*
ob *prep. with acc.* on account of
obdūco -ere -duxi -ductum draw over
obicio -ere -iēci -iectum bring upon, present

obiecto -āre -āvi -ātum expose
oblīviscor -i forget
obruo -ere -rui overwhelm
obscūrus -a -um *adj.* dark, unseen (135)
observo -āre -āvi -ātum note, trace
obsideo -ēre -sēdi -sessum besiege, blockade
obstipesco -ere -ui be astounded
obtego -ere -texi -tectum shade, conceal
obtrunco -āre -āvi -ātum slay, slaughter
occāsus -ūs *m.* downfall
occido -ere -cidi -cāsum fall, perish
occulto -āre -āvi -ātum hide, conceal
occumbo -ere -cubui -cubitum fall; yield to, succumb to (62)
oculus -i *m.* eye
ōdi *defect. verb* hate
odium -i *n.* hatred
offero -ferre obtuli oblātum offer, present; expose
ōmen -inis *n.* omen
omnipotens -entis *adj.* all-powerful
omnis -e *adj.* all, every
onus -eris *n.* burden
opācus -a -um *adj.* dark
opīmus -a -um *adj.* rich, fertile
oppōno -ere -posui -positum expose; place in the way
oppositus -a -um *adj.* opposite
ops opis *f.* hope (803); *pl.* **opēs** **opum** resources, power
opto -āre -āvi -ātum desire
opus -eris *n.* work
ōra -ae *f.* shore
ōrāculum -i *n.* oracle
orbis -is *m.* circle; coil (204)
ordo -inis *m.* row, rank, class
orior -īri orsus rise, arise
ornus -i *f.* mountain-ash

ōro -āre -āvi -ātum beg, pray

ōs ōris *n.* mouth; face; opening (482)

os ossis *n.* bone

osculum -i *n.* kiss

ostendo -ere ostendi ostensum *or* ostentum show

palma -ae *f.* palm, hand

palūs -ūdis *f.* marsh

pando -ere pandi throw open

par paris *adj.* equal to (*with dat.*)

parco -ere peperci parsum spare, curb (*with dat.*)

parens -entis *c.* parent

pāreo -ēre -ui itum obey (*with dat.*)

pariēs -etis *m.* wall of a house

pario -ere peperi partum bring forth, obtain

pariter *adv.* at the same time, together

parma -ae *f.* shield

paro -āre -āvi -ātum prepare

pars partis *f.* part; some

parvus -a -um *adj.* small

pascor -i pastus feed on, feed

passim *adv.* in all directions

passus -a -um *adj.* loose, dishevelled

passus -ūs *m.* step

pastor -ōris *m.* shepherd

patefacio -ere -fēci -factus open up

pateo -ēre -ui lie open

pater patris *m.* father

patesco -ere patui become plain

patior -i passus suffer, endure

patria -ae *f.* native land

patrius -a -um *adj.* belonging to one's father, native

paulātim *adv.* little by little

pauper -eris *adj.* poor

pavidus -a -um *adj.* trembling, fearful

pavito -āre tremble, quake

pavor -ōris *m.* dread, fear

pectus -oris *n.* heart, breast

pelagus -i *n.* sea

pellax -ācis *adj.* deceitful

pellis -is *f.* skin, hide

penātes -ium *m.* household gods

pendeo -ēre pependi hang from

penetrāle -is *n.* inner part of building

penetrālis -e *adj.* innermost

penitus *adv.* deep within

per *prep. with acc.* through, along; among (501)

pereo -īre -ii -itum perish

pererro -āre -āvi -ātum wander through

perfundo -ere -fūdi -fūsum drench

perīculum -i *n.* danger

periūrus -a -um *adj.* perjured; lying

perrumpo -ere -rūpi -ruptum break through

persolvo -ere -solvi -solūtum pay in full

persto -āre -stiti-stātum continue, persist

pervenio -īre -vēni -ventum reach, arrive

pervius -a -um *adv.* passable

pes pedis *m.* foot

peto -ere -īvi *or* -ii -ītum make for, seek

phalanx phalangis *f.* host, phalanx

pietās -tātis *f.* piety

pīneus -a -um *adj.* made of pine *or* fir

pio -āre -āvi -ātum atone for, punish (140)

placeo -ēre -ui -itum please (*with dat.*)

plāco -āre -āvi -ātum appease, pacify

plangor -ōris *m.* wailing

plurimus -a -um *adj.* very much, *pl.* very many

poena -ae *f.* punishment,
satisfaction
polus -i *m.* the heavens
pōne *adv.* behind
pōno -ere posui positum place;
shed (473)
pontus -i *m.* sea
populus -i *m.* people
porta -ae *f.* gate
porticus -ūs *m.* colonnade
posco -ere poposci demand
possum posse potui am able, can
post *adv.* afterwards
post *prep. with acc.* behind, after
postis -is *m.* doorpost
postquam *conj.* after; when
potens -entis *adj.* powerful
praeceps -cipitis *adj.* headlong
praeceps -itis *n.* a sheer drop
praeceptum -i *n.* instruction
praecipito -āre -āvi -ātum rush
headlong; throw headlong
praecipuē *adv.* especially
praecordia -ōrum *n.pl.* heart
praeda -ae *f.* booty
praemetuo -ere fear beforehand
praemium -i *n.* recompense,
reward
prehendo -ere -hendi -hensum
lay hold of, grasp
premo -ere pressi pressum press,
crush
prendo -ere prendi prensum
seize, occupy
prenso -āre -āvi -ātum grasp
prex precis *f.* prayer
prīdem *adv.* long ago, long since
prīmum *adv.* first
prīmus -a -um *adj.* first
principiō *adv.* to begin with
prius *adv.* before
prō *prep. with abl.* for
prōcēdo -ere -cessi -cessum advance

procul *adv.* far; from a distance
prōcumbo -ere -cubui -cubitum
fall forwards
prōditio -ōnis *f.* betrayal
prōdo -ere -didi -ditum betray
prōdūco -ere -dūxi -ductum
prolong
proelium -i *n.* battle
prōlābor -i -lapsus fall headlong
(555)
prōmissum -i *n.* promise
prōmitto -ere -mīsi -missum
promise
prōmo -ere prompsi promptum
bring out
prope *adv.* near
propinquo -āre -āvi -ātum approach
propinquus -a -um *adj.* near,
related
prōsequor -i -secūtus proceed,
continue
prōspicio -ere -spēxi -spectum
look ahead
prōtego -ere -tēxi -tectum protect
prōtinus *adv.* at once
prōtraho -ere -trāxi -tractum
drag forward
prōveho -ere -vēxi -vectum convey,
transport
proximus -a -um *adj.* nearest, next
pūbēs -is *f.* youth, young men
puella -ae *f.* girl
puer -i *m.* boy
pugna -ae *f.* battle
pulcher pulchra pulchrum *adj.*
beautiful
pulvis -eris *m.* dust
puppis -is *f.* stern; ship
pūrus -a -um *adj.* clear, bright
puto -āre -āvi -ātum think
quā *adv.* where
quaero -ere quaesīvi quaesītum
seek; ask about

quālis -e *adj.* such as, like
quamquam *conj.* although
quandō *adv* when; since
quantus -a -um *adj.* how much, how great
quater *adv.* three times
quatio -ere quassum shake
-que and
quī quae quod *interrog. adj.* what? which?
quī quae quod *relative pron.* who which
quia *conj.* because
quīcumque quaecumque quodcumque *pron.* whoever whatever
quid *interrog.* why?
quiēs -ētis *f.* rest, repose
quīn etiam *conj.* moreover
quīni -ae -a *distrib. adj.* five each
quinquāginta *indecl. adj.* fifty
quis qua quid *indef. adj.* some, any
quis quid *interrog. pron.* who? what?
quisquam quaequam quidquam *or* **quicquam** *pron.* anyone, anything
quisque quaeque quidque *or* **quodque** each
quisquis, quidquid *indef. pron.* whoever, whatever
quō *adv.* to where
quōcumque *adv.* wherever
quōnam *adv.* where to
quondam *adv.* once, formerly; sometimes
quot *num. adj. indecl.* as many as
rabiēs -ēi *f.* fury
rapidus -a -um *adj.* swift
rapio -ere -ui raptum seize, take
rapto -āre -āvi -ātum drag along
raptor -ōris *adj.* ravening

ratio -ōnis *f.* reckoning, reason
raucus -a -um *adj.* hoarse, hollow-sounding
recēdo -ere -cessi -cessum stand back, withdraw
recens -entis *adj.* fresh, recent
recipio -ere -cēpi -ceptum receive
recondo -ere -condidi -conditum hide, conceal
recūso -āre -āvi -ātum refuse
recutio -ere -cussi -cussum strike
reddo -ere -didi -ditum give back, restore; pay back; reply
redeo -īre redii reditum return
reditus -ūs *m.* return
redūco -ere -duxi -ductum bring back
refero -ferre -ttuli -lātum carry back; relate
reflecto -ere -flexi -flexum turn back
refugio -ere refūgi recoil
refulgeo -ēre -fulsi shine
rēgīna -ae *f.* queen
regio -ōnis *f.* direction, line
rēgius -a -um *adj.* royal
regnātor -ōris *m.* ruler
regnum -i *n.* kingdom
rēligio -ōnis *f.* religious observance; religious offering (151)
rēligiōsus -a -um *adj.* holy, sacred
relinquo -ere -līqui -lictum leave
relūceo -ere -luxi shine back, glow
remensus -a -um *perf. partic.* traversed again
remeo -āre -āvi -ātum return
remitto -ere -mīsi -missum send back
renovo -āre renew
reor rēri ratus think
repello -ere reppuli repulsum drive back

rependo -ere -pendi -pensum
pay back
repente *adv.* suddenly
repeto -ere -petīvi *or* **-petii -petītum**
seek again
repleo -ēre -plēvi -plētum fill
reporto -āre -āvi -ātum bring back
reposco -ere -posci demand,
require
reprimo -ere -pressi -pressum
check, restrain
requiesco -ere -quiēvi -quiētum
rest
requīro -ere -quīsīvi -quīsītum
inquire
rēs rei *f.* thing, matter
resideo -ēre -sēdi -sessum remain
behind
resisto -ere -stiti -stitum resist;
oppose
resolvo -ere -solvi -solūtum
undo, unbind
respicio -ere -spexi -spectum
look back
responsum -i *n.* reply
restinguo -ere -stinxi -stinctum
extinguish
resto -āre -stiti remain, be in store
retrō *adv.* backwards
revertor -i reversus return
revincio -īre -vinxi -vinctum
bind back
revīso -ere visit again
revolvo -ere -volvi -volūtum relate again, repeat
rex rēgis *m.* king
rōbur -oris *n.* timber; strength (639)
rogo -āre -āvi -ātum ask
roseus -a -um *adj.* rosy
rota -ae *f.* wheel
ruīna -ae *f.* downfall, ruin
rumpo -ere rūpi ruptum break,
burst forth

ruo -ere rui rush; tumble down
(363)
rursus *adv.* again
sacer sacra sacrum *adj.* sacred
sacerdōs -dōtis *m.* priest
sacro -āre -āvi -ātum consecrate
saepe *adv.* often
saevio -īre -ii -ītum rage
saevus -a -um *adj.* savage
salsus -a -um *adj.* salty, salted
saltus -ūs *m.* leap
salum -i *n.* sea
salūs -ūtis *f.* safety, means of safety
sanctus -a -um *adj.* holy
sanguineus -a -um *adj.* blood-red
sanguis -inis *m.* blood
saniēs -ēi *f.* saliva
sat, satis *adv.* enough
sata -ōrum *n.pl.* crops
satio -āre -āvi -ātum satisfy
satus -a -um *perf. pass. partic. of*
sero
saucius -a -um *adj.* wounded
saxum -i *n.* rock
scāla -ae *f.* ladder
scando -ere scandi scansum
climb, scale
scelerātus -a -um *adj.* profane,
impious
scelus -eris *n.* crime, wicked deed
scīlicet *adv.* of course
scindo -ere scidi scissum split,
divide
scītor -āri -ātus inquire, consult
(114)
sē *pron.* himself, herself, itself,
themselves
seco -āre secui sectum cut
sēcrētus -a -um *adj.* remote
secundus -a -um *adj.* favourable,
successful (617)
secūris -is *f.* axe
secus *adv.* otherwise

Vocabulary

sed *conj*. but

sedeo -ēre sēdi sessum sit

sēdēs -is *f.* seat, dwelling-place

seges -etis *f.* corn crop

segnitiēs *f.* sluggishness,
slowness

semper *adv.* always

senior -ōris *m.* old man

sententia -ae *f.* opinion

sentio -īre sensi sensum feel,
realise

sentis -is *m.* thorn-bush, briar

sepelio -īre sepelīvi sepultum
bury

sepulcrum -i *n.* tomb

sequor -i secūtus follow

serēnus -a -um *adj.* tranquil, serene

sero -ere sevi satum sow, beget

serpens -entis *c.* snake

serpo -ere serpsi serptum creep

sērus -a -um *adj.* late

servans -antis *adj.* observant of

servio -īre -īvi *or* -ii -ītum be a
slave to, serve (*with dat.*)

servo -āre -āvi -ātum save, keep
(789), guard (450); keep close
to (568)

sēsē *alternat. form of* se

seu...seu *or* sīve...sīve whether...or

sī *conj.* if

sībilus -a -um *adj.* hissing

sīc *adv.* thus

siccus -a -um *adj.* dry, thirsty

sīdus -eris *n.* star

signo -āre -āvi -ātum mark

signum -i *n.* sign

silentium -i *n.* silence

sileo -ēre -ui be silent

silva -ae *f.* a wood

similis -e *adj.* like

simul *adv.* at the same time

simulācrum -i *n.* image, effigy

simulo -āre -āvi -ātum pretend

sīn *conj.* but if

sine *prep. with abl.* without

sinistra -ae *f.* left hand

sino -ere sivi situm allow

sinuo -āre -āvi -ātum make to writhe

sinus -ūs *m.* bay

sisto -ere stiti statum set, place

sīve *see* seu

socer -eri *m.* father-in-law

socius -a -um *adj.* allied

socius -i *m.* ally

sōl sōlis *m.* sun

soleo -ēre solitus sum
am accustomed

solidus -a -um *adj.* firm, sound,
solid (765)

sollemnis -e *adj.* established
appointed

solum -i *n.* ground

sōlus -a -um *adj.* alone

solvo -ere solvi solūtum loosen

somnus -i *m.* sleep

sonitus -ūs *m.* sound, noise

sono -āre -ui sound, resound

sonus -i *m.* sound

sopor -ōris *m.* sleep, drowsiness

sors sortis *f.* lot

sortior -īri sortītus select

spargo -ere sparsi sparsum
scatter, spread about

speciēs -ēi *f.* sight

spēro -āre -āvi -ātum hope, hope
for expect

spēs -ēi *f.* hope

spīra -ae *f.* coil

spissus -a -um *adj.* thick

spolium -i *n.* spoil, booty

sponsus -a -um *adj.* betrothed

spūmeus -a -um *adj.* foaming

spūmo -āre -āvi -ātum foam

squāleo -ēre be rough

squāmeus -a -um *adj.* scaly

stabulum -i *n.* stall, stable

97

statio -ōnis *f.* anchorage

statuo -ere -ui -utum set up, erect

stella -ae *f.* star

sterno -ere strāvi strātum flatten, scatter

sto -āre steti statum stand

strīdo -ere -di creak

stringo -ere strinxi strictum draw (a sword)

struo -ere struxi structum devise, contrive

studium -i *n.* enthusiasm; faction (39)

stupeo -ēre be amazed, gaze in amazement at

stuppeus -a -um *adj.* made of tow

suadeo -ēre suāsi suāsum urge

sub *prep. with abl.* under

sub *prep. with acc.* under, close to (442)

subeo -īre -ii -itum come to help (216); advance (240, 725); occur to one's mind (560, 575); go under (708)

subicio -ere -iēci -iectum throw *or* place underneath

subitō *adv.* suddenly

subitus -a -um *adj.* sudden

sublābor -lābi -lapsus slip away

sublātus -a -um *pass. partic.* of **tollo**

subsisto -ere -stiti -stitum stand still, stop

succēdo -ere -cessi -cessum advance on (*with dat.*)

successus -ūs *m.* success

succurro -ere -curri -cursum run to help (*with dat.*); come to mind (317)

sūdo -āre -āvi -ātum sweat; be drenched with (582)

sūdor -ōris *m.* sweat

suffero -ferre sustuli sublātum hold up, withstand

sufficio -ere -fēci -fectum dye, tinge; supply (618)

sulcus -i *m.* furrow, trail

sulphur -uris *n.* sulphur

sum esse fui be

summus -a -um *adj.* highest, top of; greatest

sūmo -ere sumpsi sumptum take, exact; take up

super *adv.* in addition, moreover; on top

super *prep. with acc.* over, above

superbus -a -um *adj.* proud

supero -āre -āvi -ātum rise above; survive (597, 643)

supersum -esse -fui be left over, survive

superus -a -um *adj.* upper, higher

supplex -icis *c.* suppliant

suprēmus -a -um *adj.* last

surgo -ere surrēxi surrectum rise

suscito -āre -āvi -ātum stir up, rouse

suspectus -a -um *adj.* suspect

suspensus -a -um *adj.* doubtful, in suspense

suus -a -um *adj.* his/her/its/their own

tabulātum -i *n.* floor, storey

taceo -ēre -ui -itum am silent

tacitus -a -um *adj.* quiet, silent

tactus -ūs *m.* touch

talis -e *adj.* such

tam *adv.* so, such

tamen *adv.* however, yet

tandem *adv.* at last

tantum *adv.* only

tantus -a -um *adj.* so great, such great

tardus -a -um *adj.* slow

taurus -i *m.* bull

tectum -i *n.* roof; building

tego -ere texi tectum cover, hide, protect (430)

tellūs -ūris *f.* land

tēlum -i *n.* weapon

tempero -āre -āvi -ātum refrain

tempestās -tātis *f.* storm

templum -i *n.* temple

tempto -āre -āvi -ātum test, try

tempus -oris *n.* time; *in pl.*
temples of the head (133, 684)

tendo -ere tetendi tensum *or*
tentum stretch out; strive;
(*with* ad) make for; encamp (29)

tenebrae -ārum *f.pl.* darkness

teneo -ēre tenui tentum hold;
restrain; occupy

tener -era -erum *adj.* tender

tenuis -e *adj.* thin

tenus *prep. with abl.* as far as
(*generally follows its noun*)

ter *adv.* three times

terebro -āre -āvi -ātum bore a hole

tergum -i *n.* back

terra -ae *f.* land, earth

terreo -ēre -ui -itum frighten

testor -āri testātus call to witness

testūdo -inis *f.* tortoise, name
given to a body of troops
advancing with shields held
over their heads.

texo -ere texui textum weave, fit
together

thalamus -i *m.* bedroom

timeo -ēre -ui fear

tollo -ere sustuli sublātum raise

torrens -entis *m.* torrent

torus -i *m.* couch

tot *indecl. adj.* so many

totiens *adv.* so many times,
so often

tōtus -a -um *adj.* whole

trabs trabis *f.* beam; panel (481)

traho -ere traxi tractum drag

traicio -ere -iēci -iectum pierce

tranquillus -a -um *adj.* calm

transfero -ferre -tuli -lātum
transfer

tremefacio -ere -fēci -factum
make to tremble

tremendus -a -um *adj.* terrible

tremo -ere -ui tremble, quiver (52)

tremor -ōris *m.* trembling

trepido -āre -āvi -ātum tremble

trepidus -a -um *adj.* trembling

tridens -entis *m.* trident

tristis -e *adj.* sad; grim

trisulcus -a -um *adj.* triple-forked

triumphus -i *m.* triumph

trucīdo -āre -āvi -ātum slaughter

truncus -i *m.* trunk; headless corpse

tu *pron.* you (*sing.*)

tuba -ae *f.* trumpet

tueor -ēri tuitus look at, view
(604); protect

tum *adv.* then

tumeo -ēre swell

tumidus -a -um *adj.* swollen

tumultus -ūs *m.* uproar

tumulus -i *m.* mound

tunc *adv.* then

turba -ae *f.* crowd

turbo -āre -āvi -ātum agitate,
confuse

turbo -inis *m.* whirlwind

turpis -e *adj.* disgraceful

turris -is *f.* tower

tūtor -āri tutātus guard, protect

tūtus -a -um *adj.* safe

tuus -a -um *adj.* your

ubi *conj.* when; where

ubīque *adv.* everywhere

ulciscor -i ultus avenge

ullus -a -um *adj.* any

ultimus -a -um *adj.* last, final

ultor -ōris *m.* avenger

ultrix -trīcis *adj.* avenging

ultrō *adv.* of one's own accord

ululo -āre -āvi -ātum howl, shriek

ulva -ae *f.* sedge
umbo -ōnis *m.* boss of a shield
umbra -ae *f.* shadow
umerus -i *m.* shoulder
ūmidus -a -um *adj.* damp
umquam *adv.* ever
ūnā *adv.* at same time, together
unda -ae *f.* wave
unde *adv.* from where
undique *adv.* from all sides
undo -āre -āvi -ātum billow
ūnus -a -um *adj.* one
urbs urbis *f.* city
urgeo -ēre ursi press hard on
ūro -ere ussi ustum burn
usquam *adv.* anywhere
usque *adv.* constantly, continually
ūsus -ūs *m.* use, usage
ut *conj.with indic.* as, when; how
  (283); *with subj.* how (4), so
  that, that (434, 665)
uterque utraque utrumque
  pron. and adj. each (of two)
uterus -i *m.* belly, womb
utī *alternat. form of* ut
utinam *adv. with subj.* would that
vacuus -a -um *adj.* empty
vādo -ere go
vagor -āri vagātus go about,
  wander
valē (*imperat.*) farewell
valeo -ēre -ui -itum be strong,
  be able
validus -a -um *adj.* strong,
  mighty
vallis -is *f.* valley
vānus -a -um *adj.* empty, false
varius -a -um *adj.* various
vastus -a -um *adj.* immense
vātēs -is *c.* soothsayer, prophet
-ve *conj.* or
vel *conj.* or
vello -ere velli vulsum tear away

vēlo -āre -āvi -ātum cover, wrap
vēlum -i *n.* sail
velutī *adv.* just as, like
venēnum -i *n.* poison
venio -īre vēni ventum come
venter -tris *m.* belly
ventus -i *m.* wind
verbum -i *n.* word
vērō *adv.* indeed
verso -āre -āvi -ātum carry on
vertex -icis *m.* top, summit
verto -ere verti versum turn,
  overturn
vērum -i *n.* truth
vērus -a -um *adj.* true
vester -ra -rum *adj.* your
vestibulum -i *n.* entrance-court
vestīgium -i *n.* footprint
vestis -is *f.* garment
veto -āre vetui vetitum, oppose,
  forbid
vetus -eris *adj.* old
vetustus -a -um *adj.* old, ancient
via -ae *f.* street, path
vibro -āre -āvi -ātum flicker
vicēs *f.pl.* answering blows
victor -ōris *adj.* victorious
victor -ōris *m.* conqueror
victōria -ae *f.* victory
video -ēre vīdi vīsum see; *in pass.*
  seem
vigeo -ēre flourish, be of high repute
vigil -is *m.* sentinel
vinclum -i *n.* chain
vinco -ere vīci victum conquer
vinculum -i *n.* chain
vīnum -i *n.* wine
violābilis -e *adj.* that may be defiled
violo -āre -āvi -ātum defile
vir viri *m.* man
vīrēs -ium *f.pl.* strength
virgineus -a -um *adj.* belonging
  to a virgin

virgō -inis *f.* maiden, virgin
virtūs -tūtis *f.* courage
vīs *acc.* **vim** *abl.* **vī** *f.* force, vigor
vīso -ere vīsi vīsum to look at
vīsus -ūs *m.* sight
vīta -ae *f.* life
vīto -āre -āvi -ātum avoid
vitta -ae *f.* sacred fillet,
  headband
vīvus -a -um *adj.* alive; running
  (719)
vix *adv.* with difficulty, scarcely
vōciferor -āri vociferātus
  cry out
voco -āre -āvi -ātum call
volo velle volui wish
volucer -cris -cre *adj.* swift
volūmen -inis *n.* fold
volvo -ere volvi volūtum roll
vōs *pron.* you (*plur.*)
vōtum -i *n.* votive offering
vox vōcis *f.* voice, word
vulgus -i *n.* the common people;
  throng (798)
vulnus -eris *n.* wound
vultus -ūs *m.* face

PROPER NAMES

Acamas -antis *m.* — Acamas, a Greek warrior
Achāicus -a -um *adj.* — Greek
Achilles -is *and* -i *m.* — Achilles, son of Peleus king of Thessaly and the greatest warrior in the Greek army
Achīvī -orum *m.pl.* — Achaeans, i.e. Greeks
Aenēas -ae *m.* — son of Venus and Anchises. Mythical ancestor of the Romans
Aiax -ācis *m.* — Ajax, a Greek warrior and king of the Locrians
Anchīsēs -ae *m.* — Anchises, father of Aeneas
Androgeōs -ei *m.* — Androgeos, a Greek
Andromachē -ēs *f.* — Andromache, wife of Hector
Apollo -inis *m.* — the god Apollo
Argī -ōrum *m.pl.* — Argos, chief city of the Argolid in southern Greece
Argīvus -a -um *adj.* — of Argos, Argive, i.e. Greek
Argolicus -a -um *adj.* — Greek
Argos *n.* — Argos, chief city of the Argolid in southern Greece
Ascanius -i *m.* — Ascanius, son of Aeneas and Creusa, also called Iulus
Asia -ae *f.* — Asia Minor
Astyanax -actis *m.* — Astyanax, son of Hector and Andromache
Atrīdae -ārum *m.pl.* — sons of Atreus, i.e. Agamemnon and Menelaus
Auster -stri *m.* — the south wind
Automedōn -ontis *m.* — Automedon, the charioteer of Achilles
Bēlīdēs -ae *m.* — descendant of Belus, Palamedes
Calchās -antis *m.* — Calchas, soothsayer of the Greek army
Capys -yos m. — Capys, a Trojan
Cassandra -ae *f.* — Cassandra, daughter of Priam and Hecuba
Cerēs -eris *f.* — Ceres, goddess of corn
Coroebus -i *m.* — Coroebus, a Trojan suitor of Cassandra
Creūsa -ae *f.* — Creusa, daughter of Priam and wife of Aeneas
Danaī -ōrum *m.pl.* — the Greeks, descendants of Danaus founder of Argos

Dardania -ae *f.*	Troy
Dardanidae -ārum/-um *m.*	the Trojans, descendants of Dardanus
Dardanis -idis *f.*	a Trojan woman
Dardanius -a -um *adj.*	Trojan
Dardanus -a -um *adj.*	Trojan
Dēiphobus -i *m.*	Deiphobus, a son of Priam
Dolopēs -um *m.pl.*	the Dolopes, a people of Thessaly in Greece
Dōricus -a -um *adj.*	Doric, i.e. Greek
Dymas -antis *m.*	Dymas, a Trojan
Eōus -a -um *adj.*	eastern, of the morning
Epēos -i *m.*	Epeos, the Greek who devised the wooden horse
Epytus -i *m.*	Epytus, a Trojan
Erīnys -yos *f.*	a Fury
Eurus -i m.	the south-east wind
Eurypylus -i *m.*	Greek sent to consult the oracle of Apollo
Fortūna -ae *f.*	the goddess Fortune
Gorgō -onis *f.*	the Gorgon Medusa
Grāii -ōrum *m.pl.*	the Greeks
Grāius -a -um *adj.*	Greek
Hector -oris *m.*	Hector, eldest son of Priam and Hecuba
Hectoreus -a -um *adj.*	belonging to Hector
Hecuba -ae *f.*	Hecuba, the wife of Priam
Hesperius -a -um *adj.*	western
Hypanis -is *m.*	Hypanis, a Trojan
Īda -ae *f.*	Ida, a mountain
Īdaeus -a -um *adj.*	of Ida, a mountain near Troy
Īliacus -a -um *adj.*	Trojan
Īliadēs -um *f.pl.*	Trojan women
Īlium -i *n.*	Troy
Īphitus -i *m.*	Iphitus, a Trojan
Ithacus -a -um *adj.*	Ithacan, of Ithaca a Greek island in the Ionian sea
Īulus -i *m.*	Iulus, son of Aeneas and Creusa, also called Ascanius
Iūnō -ōnis *f.*	the goddess Juno, wife of Jupiter
Iūppiter, Iovis *m.*	Jupiter, king of the gods
Lacaenus -a -um *adj.*	Spartan
Lāocoōn -ontis *m.*	Laocoon, priest of Apollo in Troy
Lārissaeus -a -um *adj.*	of Larissa a city of Thessaly in northern Greece

103

Lūcifer -eri *m.*	morning-star
Lȳdius -a -um *adj.*	Lydian
Machāon -onis *m.*	Machaon, son of Aesculapius, a Greek warrior
Mars Martis *m.*	Mars, god of war
Menelāus -i *m.*	Menelaus, brother of Agamemnon and king of Sparta
Minerva -ae *f.*	Minerva, goddess of wisdom
Mycēnae -arum *f.pl.*	Mycenae, a fortress in southern Greece and home of Agamemnon.
Mygdonides -ae *m.*	son of Mygdon; see Coroebus
Myrmidones -um *m.pl.*	the Myrmidons, a people of Thessaly in Greece
Neoptolemus -i *m.*	Neoptolemus, son of Achilles, also called Pyrrhus
Neptūnius -a -um *adj.*	of Neptune
Neptūnus -i *m.*	Neptune, god of the sea
Nēreūs -i *m.*	Nereus, a sea god
Notus -i *m.*	the south wind
Ōceanus -i *m.*	the ocean
Olympus -i m.	Olympus, a mountain in Greece and home of the gods
Orcus -i *m.*	Orcus, a name for the underworld
Othryades -ae *m.*	son of Othrys; see Panthus
Palamēdes -is *m.*	Palamedes, son of king Nauplius
Palladium -i *n.*	image of Pallas Athene
Pallas -adis *f.*	Pallas, a title of Athene who was identified by the Romans with Minerva
Panthūs -i *m.*	Panthus, a priest of Apollo at Troy
Paris -idis *m.*	Paris, son of Priam and Hecuba
Pelasgi -ōrum *m.pl.*	Pelasgi, the oldest inhabitants of Greece; the Greeks
Pelasgus -a -um *adj.*	Pelasgan, i.e. Greek
Peliās -ae *m.*	Pelias, a Trojan
Pēlīdes -ae *m.*	son or grandson of Peleus, i.e. Achilles or Neoptolemus
Pelopēus -a -um *adj.*	of Pelops, i.e. Greek
Pēneleus -ei *m.*	Peneleus, a Greek leader
Pergama -ōrum *n.pl.*	the citadel of Troy
Periphas -antis *m.*	Periphas, a Greek comrade of Pyrrhus